Texts That Linger
Words That Explode

Texts That Linger
Words That Explode

Listening to Prophetic Voices

WALTER BRUEGGEMANN

edited by Patrick D. Miller

FORTRESS PRESS

Minneapolis

TEXTS THAT LINGER, WORDS THAT EXPLODE
Listening to Prophetic Voices

Cover photo copyright © 1999 Photodisc, Inc.
Cover design: Craig Claeys
Interior design: Beth Wright

Library of Congress Cataloging-in-Publication Data

Brueggemann, Walter.
    Texts that linger, words that explode : listening to prophetic voices / Walter Brueggemann ; edited by Patrick D. Miller.
        p. cm.
    Includes bibliographical references and index.
    ISBN 0-8006-3231-1 (pbk.)
    1. Bible. O.T.—Criticism, interpretation, etc. 2. Prophecy—Judaism.
    I. Miller, Patrick D. II. Title.
BS1198 .B6318 2000
221.6—dc21   99-047465

The paper used in this publication meets the minimum requirements of American National Standard for Information Sciences — Permanence of Paper for Printed Library Materials, ANSI Z329.48-1984.

Manufactured in the U.S.A.   AF 1-3231
04   03   02   01   00   2   3   4   5   6   7   8   9   10

Contents

Editor's Foreword

WHILE HE HAS WRITTEN MANY BOOKS ON MANY BIBLICAL TOPICS, WALTER Brueggemann is as well known for his more ad hoc essays of both scholarly and popular character. A number of these from the earlier years of his writing were gathered together in three volumes published in the first half of this decade.[1] Now a second series is under way comprising a number—but only a part—of the academic and ecclesial essays he has written in more recent years. Many of these originated in oral form, reflecting Brueggemann's widespread popularity as a lecturer: both in the guild of biblical scholarship and among pastors and lay people in the church. He is an orator in the classical sense, and the emphasis on rhetoric that comes to play in his *Theology of the Old Testament*—and will be the focus of attention in the final volume of this series—is everywhere evident in his speaking and writing. It seems impossible for him to write in a pedestrian or purely academic manner without beginning to exhort or to drop a rhetorical shoe with a loud thud behind the unsuspecting listener/reader who may have expected that this time Brueggemann is just going to do some exegesis without disturbing anybody or suggesting that the text has something radically to do with the life and faith of the reader. That rhetorical punch is about as characteristic of his essays in the *Journal of Biblical Literature* as it is of those that appear in *The Christian Century* or the *Journal for Preachers*. The fact that he is an editor of this last journal speaks volumes about where he thinks the real action is.

In the first volume of this new series of collected essays, Brueggemann dealt with covenant and its implications for human and, more particularly, Christian existence.[2] The second volume returns to a part of Scripture that has occupied his attention from the beginning of his academic career and has continued to be for him a rich mine of inquiry and productive interpretation: *the prophets*. His first scholarly essay was a study of Amos 4, and his first scholarly book was a study of Hosea.[3] His little book *The Prophetic Imagination* has sold tens of thousands of copies and remains one of the most perceptive uncoverings of the prophetic voice in contemporary Old Testament study.

The prophet Jeremiah has particularly occupied his attention, and one suspects the concentration on this prophet's message may be because Brueggemann sees so clearly in the Book of Jeremiah a resonance with contemporary society and the church, both under the threat of judgment in the face of a large indifference to the demands of justice and love and assuming that surface commitments are sufficient to allow us to pursue mammon—in

Jeremiah called Baal—and "profit" (see Jer. 2:8, 11). Brueggemann's commentary on Jeremiah is a masterful integration of social, political, and theological insight into the message of that book.[4]

The title of this volume is taken from the first essay, "Texts that Linger, Words that Explode," an apt description not only of the content of the essay but of Brueggemann's way of working, his capacity to take long familiar passages of Scripture and uncover their power in fresh ways. As always, texts are in view. But the line between then and now is never sharp in his interpretive work, in this instance marvelously demonstrated by the connections Brueggemann makes between the text about Rachel's weeping over her children and Jonathan Kozol's book on homelessness in New York, titled *Rachel and Her Children*. The explosion is always that of the text, but it is the text as ignited by Brueggemann that flares up so powerfully.

In a similar way, Brueggemann takes up a number of texts in the Book of Isaiah—the other prophet on which he has written a commentary—and shows how they linger on in the tradition and come to life or explode afresh in different times and circumstances ("Five Strong Rereadings of the Book of Isaiah"). This is an exercise in the *Wirkungsgeschichte* of the biblical text. His point, however, is not simply to illustrate the history of reception of the texts but to show how texts in a particular prophetic book "perform in human society," how they stand "in the service of protest on the side of transformation."

Yet another text, this time one that generally lies dormant in Scripture, is revealed to have a genuinely explosive potential to shatter some of the most treasured components of the biblical tradition. It is Amos' brief verse in 9:7, which suggests that the Lord of Israel has other stories than just the one with and about Israel, other redemptive and formative events, than just the one Israel knows ("'Exodus' in the Plural"). Revealing the subversive character of this text, he uncovers the way it challenges the ideology of election that assumes we are special and all the others are "other" to God also. Not so, says Amos, and Brueggemann agrees, in the process exploding the monopolistic tendencies of both Jews and Christians where they are present.

This essay on Amos 9:7 joins with two other essays—"The Scandal and Liberty of Particularity" and "Always in the Shadow of the Empire"—to think about the story of Israel in relation to other nations and peoples. But the burr that Amos hides under the saddle of triumphalism is set alongside a quite different kind of experience, the domination of Israel by various empires throughout its history. Here Brueggemann explores the meaning of Israel's particularity and the way that people-nation functioned, in reality and in ideal, as a kind of counter-community to the dominant powers of their time. The point of this examination of how Israel lived in the shadow of Egypt, Assyria, Babylonia, and Persia is to learn from it the urgency of attending to the peculiar narrative identity of the church in a time when that identity is constantly succumbing to secularism.

More surprising than any of the above is Brueggemann's focus upon the figure of Baruch in the Book of Jeremiah ("The 'Baruch Connection': Reflections on Jer. 43:1-7"). His interest is not so much in reconstructing a historical profile of Jeremiah's amanuensis or even in figuring out what parts of the book may be assigned to Baruch. Rather, he finds in the texts around Baruch both some lessons in the interplay of ideology and utopia, a la Karl Mannheim, Frederic Jameson, and Paul Ricoeur, and some clues to the coherence and canonical shaping of the book of Jeremiah.[5]

These probings into ancient texts and contemporary consciousness are an invitation to the reader to return to the texts and to let their words explode once more. It may not be a pleasant experience. I am often struck by how readily people listen to Brueggemann and read his books. For this contemporary prophet does not mince words or preach comfortable sermons. There is an abrasiveness that comes from an authentic hearing of the word. Maybe the response of his listeners is itself a testimony, not to the popularity of a writer/speaker but to the power of the Scriptures he interprets and their compelling call, even when they place us under the threat of judgment.

Patrick D. Miller

Notes

1. *Old Testament Theology: Essays on Structure, Theme, and Text*, ed. Patrick D. Miller (Minneapolis: Fortress Press, 1992); *A Social Reading of the Old Testament: Prophetic Approaches to Israel's Communal Life*, ed. Patrick D. Miller (Minneapolis: Fortress Press, 1994); *The Psalms and the Life of Faith*, ed. Patrick D. Miller (Minneapolis: Fortress Press, 1995). In addition to these volumes, several previously published essays appeared in *Cadences of Home: Preaching among Exiles* (Louisville: Westminster John Knox, 1997), and a collection of his sermons has been published with the title *The Threat of Life: Sermons on Pain, Power, and Weakness*, ed. Charles L. Campbell (Minneapolis: Fortress Press, 1996).

2. See the Preface to *The Covenanted Self: Explorations in Law and Covenant*, ed. Patrick D. Miller (Minneapolis: Fortress Press, 1999), vii–ix.

3. For a bibliography of Brueggemann's writings, see the volume of essays published in his honor titled *God in the Fray: A Tribute to Walter Brueggemann*, ed. Tod Linafelt and Timothy K. Beal (Minneapolis: Fortress Press, 1998), 321–40.

4. *A Commentary on Jeremiah: Exile and Homecoming* (Grand Rapids: Eerdmans, 1998).

5. This discussion of Baruch's significance for the Book of Jeremiah is carried further in Brueggemann's commentary on Jeremiah.

Preface

THE INTERPRETATION OF PROPHETIC TEXTS IS ENDLESSLY CHALLENGING and problematic. It is unmistakably clear that these ancient texts continue to have compelling power for us. At the same time, the texts do not readily and easily lend themselves to any contemporary "application." These several essays reflect my attempt to engage the prophetic texts, all the while being mindful of the endless challenge. These papers of course did not need to be republished in this form. I do so in the hope that they may be of some value as others grapple with the challenge, with the chance and temptation of contemporaneity. Continued focus on such ancient rootage is surely urgent among us given the deep places of old failure and new gifts that are everywhere evident among us.

I am glad to thank, yet again, the "usual suspects," that make my work possible. That number includes Tim Simpson, who again helped transform these sundry pages into a book form; Patrick Miller who not only lends the book his support by way of a foreword, but also worked at selecting and ordering the pieces included; and a host of generous people at Fortress Press who have been endlessly supportive, in this case K. C. Hanson and long-term Michael West but also others at the press who make a difference to those of us who find our way to Fortress. Finally and always, Tempie Alexander manages projects like this one and the larger project of my working life with finesse and shrewdness matched by long-suffering patience. On all these counts I am deeply grateful.

Walter Brueggemann
Epiphany 2000

Texts That Linger, Words That Explode

> The true meaning of scripture is the solid historical reality of the
> continuum of actual meanings over the centuries to actual people. It
> is as mundane, or as transcending, or both, as have been those actual
> meanings in the lives and hearts of persons. . . . The scripture . . . is
> dimly or vividly recognized as meaning not only such-and-such but
> at the same time more even than that, more than the reader or hearer
> has as yet discerned.
>
> *Wilfred Cantwell Smith*, What Is Scripture?
> A Comparative Approach (*Fortress Press, 1993, 89*)

THE DURABLE ROLE OF BIBLICAL TEXT AS AVAILABLE TRADITION, WHICH
the community tends always to utter and experience again, is not done,
characteristically, either with a full-blown *canonical* awareness or with a
full-blown *critical* awareness. Rather, the force of these texts, which continue
to sound in text, is through ad hoc use, utterance out of dense memory long
schooled in the text in which an imaginative re-utterance makes poignant,
astonishing, compelling, and illuminating but ad hoc contact with the present moment of experience.

In this subsequent moment of re-utterance and rehearing, both the
speaker (quoter) and the hearer recognize intuitively that this is "the right
text" in this moment, even if it is taken out of canonical or critical context.
In that moment of utterance, the text is offered by the speaker (quoter) and
received by the listener as revelatory. That is, it discloses something about
this moment that would, without this utterance, not be known, seen, heard,
or made available. It is, in my judgment, this ad hoc quality of text reuse,
given in courageous imagination and received by intuition, which has been
lacking in much of the conflicted discussion about canon and criticism.

It is the work of *canonical* practice in ecclesial communities and the
work of *criticism* in the scholarly community to keep the text available. It
is by the ongoing enterprise of religious and scholarly communities that the
text lingers over time in available ways. Out of that lingering, however,
from time to time, words of the text characteristically erupt into new usage.
They are seized upon by someone in the community with daring. Or perhaps better, the words of the text seize someone in the community who is a
candidate for daring. In that moment of re-utterance, the present is freshly
illuminated, reality is irreversibly transformed. The community comes to
know or see or receive or decide afresh. What has been *tradition,* hovering
in dormancy, becomes available *experience.* In the moment of speaking and

hearing, this is treasured tradition now become present experience, inimitable, without parallel, irreversible. In that utterance, the word does lead reality.

In what follows, I will consider several examples from the book of Jeremiah of the way in which these lingerings of tradition become explosions of utterance that make the world oddly different in the present.

I will pay attention to the ways in which these texts exercise ongoing influence in the community of faith well beyond their primary utterance in the book of Jeremiah.

1

The first of these is in Jer. 2:6-8a:

> They did not say, "Where is the LORD
>   who brought us up from the land of Egypt,
> who led us in the wilderness,
>   in a land of deserts and pits,
> in a land of drought and deep darkness,
>   in a land that no one passes through,
>   where no one lives?"
> I brought you into a plentiful land
>   to eat its fruit and its good things.
> But when you entered you defiled my land,
>   and made my heritage an abomination.
> The priests did not say, "Where is the LORD?"

These verses form a centerpiece in the larger text of vv. 4-13, which scholars have widely recognized to be a "lawsuit" speech. They are an indictment, a statement of Israel's guilt that justifies the punishment of Yahweh soon to be inflicted.

These verses are organized around two parallel indictments, "They did not say . . . " (vv. 6, 8). It is interesting and important that Israel is indicted here not for what it did not do, but for what it did not say. The indictment recognizes that Israel is essentially a community of utterance. When Israel ceases to utter rightly, the community is jeopardized. In the first indictment, the entire community is accused, the explicit subject being "your ancestors." The phrase refers here to all the past generations of Israel from Moses to the time of Jeremiah. All of them are indicted for a failure to "say." What they did not say pertains to Yahweh's deliverance from Egypt and Yahweh's safe leadership in the wilderness. The long line of ancestors did not publicly—out loud—give an account of the ways in which Yahweh's faithful, powerful presence made life possible for Israel. They neglected to say, or they forgot to say, and in their failure to say, Yahweh, the central character of Israel's past, disappeared—so that a failure to say leads to a sense of autonomy, a life without Yahweh.

The indictment is only "they did not say." We notice that there is no indirect object. They did not say to whom? We might expect that they did not say to their children. Or perhaps to their nonbelieving neighbors. But then perhaps the point is not that they did not speak so that somebody did not hear who needed to hear. It is as plausible that Israel needed to say. It is the saying, not the hearing, that matters here, for it is the saying that keeps the speakers inside the story, just as the saying keeps Yahweh palpably at the center of Israel's narrative and identity.

The second indictment for "not saying" (v. 8) pertains to the priests. It is much briefer and appears to be a subset of the first "not say" indictment. That is, the priests did not name the name, make available—out loud—the One who is the key actor in Israel's core story.

This text from Jeremiah, so far as I know, is nowhere later explicitly cited. I mention it here because it suggests to me four facets of the tradition that continue to be reexperienced.

1. Our primary concern is the way in which Jeremiah texts are generative later on. In this case, however, we can see that "Jeremiah" is on the receiving end of the traditioning process already long underway in Israel. That is, Jeremiah takes up and appeals to what appears to be an already stylized formulation. This reuse is an ongoing processive matter, and text makers are always "on the way," perhaps never at the beginning of a text or at the end of text making, but knowing themselves to be members and participants in the larger enterprise.

2. This text makes evident that Israel is primarily a community of utterance. Israel engages in narrative recital that is a form of testimony. And the testimony is *advocacy* for a certain rendering of reality and a *polemic* against other renderings of reality, in this case, renderings of reality that omit mention of Yahweh as a key actor. It is clear that Israel is to be a community of obedience; one particular aspect of that obedience is obedient speech. If we continue in chapter 2, we can see that speech is enormously important for the speaker, for the speaker catalogues all the things Israel has said that are acts of disloyalty and disobedience:

> You said, "I will not serve!" (v. 19)
> How can you say, I am not defiled . . . ?" (v. 23)
> But you said, "It is hopeless . . ." (v. 25)
> They say, "Come and save us!" (v. 27)
> My people say, "We are free." (v. 31)
> You say, "I am innocent . . . I have not sinned." (v. 35)

3. This text suggests a stylized recital as a sine qua non for Israel, a recital that must not be unlike the one out of which Gerhard von Rad organized his theology.[1] That recital is of course supple. But it also has

features of constancy, among which are "saving events" that are said to have Yahweh as their subject. The text suggests a notion of an ongoing, fixed recital that was indispensable for Israel's life. Some in Israel, at least, perhaps the "Yahweh alone party," believed that getting the story straight was a primary responsibility for the well-being of the community, and even for the security of the state.[2] The only way to get the story straight, moreover, is to say it out loud in public repeatedly.

4. The failure to get the story straight has inordinately negative consequences for Israel. The tradition of Jeremiah in general is preoccupied with the consequences, which come to fruition in the Babylonian seizure of Jerusalem. More pointedly, the conclusion of Jer. 2:36-37 quite concretely anticipates a terrible outcome for Judah.

Thus the text lingers over right speech and the cost of the failure to speak aright. There is an opening here to something like a creedal tradition, one that is not authoritarian, but one that ensures "getting the story straight." The danger in Israel is that Israel would lose its normative story as they "went after things that do not profit" (v. 8). The outcome was a failed autonomy. Were this text now to explode in contemporaneity, it might make contact with a religious community that has not got its story straight, either in liberal indifference or in conservative reductionism.[3] And the failure to say rightly, the pursuit of loyalties that do not profit, ends, it might be argued, with the verdict, "You will not prosper through them" (v. 37).

II

The second text I take up has more subsequent, concrete use. When the tradition reflects upon failed Jerusalem, either anticipated failure or failure in fact, it is driven to massive, unguarded grief (compare the book of Lamentations; 2 Chron. 35:20; Neh. 1:4; Ps. 137:1). And when the tradition of Jeremiah wants to articulate this unrestrained grief most fully, it recruits mother Rachel, from Genesis, to lead the voicing of grief:

> A voice is heard in Ramah,
>   lamentation and bitter weeping.
> Rachel is weeping for her children;
>   she refuses to be comforted for her children,
>   because they are not. (Jer. 31:15)

Again, the Jeremiah tradition is on the receiving end of the traditioning process, for its poetry clearly appeals back to Genesis. In Gen. 37, with the alleged death of Joseph, it is father Jacob, not mother Rachel, who "refused to be comforted" (v. 35).[4] In taking over this tradition of grief for the loss of the beloved from Genesis, however, the refusal of comfort has been reassigned to mother Rachel. The Genesis text has lingered, and now it explodes in the tradition of Jeremiah.

It explodes in remarkable imagination. This imaginative act is remarkable because of the transference of grief to mother Rachel, for mother, in that ancient world as in the contemporary world, can characteristically grieve more effusively for lost, treasured sons than can anyone else. The imaginative act of transference, however, is more than this. It is that the Jacob-Rachel-Joseph reference from Genesis should be used at all in this new context. That old story apparently had lingered in Israel's memory, and now it erupts with odd poignancy. In the poetic scenario in Jeremiah where mother Rachel makes her belated reappearance, the tradition mobilizes the entire history of the ancestors, all the long-gone witnesses who watch over Israel in caring, enduring anxiety.

Now the ancestors watch while this Israel suffers grief, humiliation, and death. The old lady and all her people are inconsolable. The loss of Jerusalem is not simply a geopolitical inevitability, or a mistake among the Jerusalem kings. It is a cosmic loss, so far as we know, completely irreversible. The poet refuses to reason about the loss, for this loss is beyond all rationality. The poet intends that the hearer shall enter into the grief, enter it and grieve with mother Rachel and "refuse to be comforted." It is no wonder that Rachel occupies such a prominent position in the ongoing lore of Judaism, all the way from 587 until the Holocaust.[5] This mother lingers with her sobs in the midst of Israel. Mother Rachel can linger so palpably, so long, so well, only because this poet has given us these lines with their great, poignant durability. Mother Rachel is available for grieved Israel because of this courageous act of text making that makes her available.

We may mention three subsequent uses of this text, which lingers until it explodes.

1. In the Gospel account of Matthew, the narrative spends time on the events around the birth of Jesus and the visit of the Wise Men from the east. Matthew locates the narrative in the midst of the brutality and in the midst of international politics. At the center of that brutality is the villain and nemesis Herod. Herod is Pharaoh revisited from Exodus. The telling of the Jesus story is the retelling of the story of Israel. There is Egypt again, and much killing of children. And then there is the flight to safety in "the land of Israel" (Matt. 2:21).

In the middle of that account of irrational brutality at the hands of this new pharaoh, all fixed upon exodus topology, Jeremiah's Rachel text explodes once again:

> A voice is heard in Ramah
>   wailing and loud lamentations,
> Rachel weeping for her children;
>   she refuses to be consoled, because they are no more.
> (Matt. 2:18)

What an odd usage! Matthew did not need to quote this text, was not
scripted to do so. Except that in a moment of imaginative courage, the
action of Pharaoh in Egypt and the later action of Nebuchadnezzar against
Jerusalem converge. The gospel writer imagines that this brutality is like
those two brutalities. Indeed, they are all of a piece. They are all there—
Pharaoh, Nebuchadnezzar, Herod—enemies of Israel, and enemies of God's
gift of newness, which they crush in deathliness.

And so mother Rachel and all her grieving companions must be routed
out one more time. This is a new grief, a depth of grief never known
before in Israel. And yet this grief is of a piece with the previous loss in
Genesis and the lost city in Jeremiah. Indeed, this is a treasured people
always at risk and always brutalized. Nothing will do now, except to
"refuse to be comforted." And in the reuse of that tradition, the grief is
reexperienced in all its depth, a grief that foreshadowed all the hurt that
will come to its accursed Friday. And Rachel will sob yet more deeply as
she is "son-forsaken."[6]

2. Rachel lingers, so Samuel Dresner observes, in an isolated tomb all
alone outside Jerusalem, away from her dead ancestral colleagues who are
all gathered in Hebron. Rachel lingers not only in her lonely tomb, but also
in the midrashic tradition, the mother of all grief. She is there alone in her
tomb, alive in the tradition. And then she is summoned, belatedly, by Emil
Fackenheim.[7] That great meditator upon the Holocaust concludes that
Rachel has good reason to refuse to be comforted. She finds her grief too
deep and her sadness too bitter, grief over Jerusalem, deeper sadness over
Auschwitz. For says Fackenheim, Rachel had six million children, and now
they are all dead. Mother Rachel cannot cease her trembling, shattering
sobbing ever, because the children are never forgotten and never given up.
It is the hard work of mothering always to remember:

> Even these may forget; yet I will never forget you. (Isa. 49:15)

Did Rachel in Genesis know about the holocaust to come? Did Rachel in
Jeremiah know about the pending Shoah? Did the poet in Jeremiah anticipate the ovens? Well, no, of course not. Except, except that these are all
Jews . . . mother Rachel, the oven-destined, and the poet. Auschwitz, moreover, is very close to Ramah. And therefore the same texts will do.

3. Jonathan Kozol, that troublesome gadfly, has written a gruesome
book on the homeless in New York City. He describes, in unbearable detail,
the ways in which these "surplus people" are warehoused in hotels, which
appears to be "the final solution." Kozol takes up one case study of a mother with children, who lives in the brutalizing hotel, completely unsafe, ominous, at risk, without resources. His book is an unrelenting exposé. Oddly
the mother in this case study is named Rachel. Is that her real name? And
the book is entitled *Rachel and Her Children*.[8] Is that an accident? Did
Kozol push to the right mother until he found a Rachel? Or did he invent

her? Or are all desperate mothers inevitably named Rachel? Well, Kozol is a Jew. What else could he name her? He could not name her anything else. Kozol stays outside religion in his exposé, for this is a story of failed economics. He steps outside Jewishness, for this is, in large measure, a gentile surplus.

But the name Rachel is available for the telling. Mother Rachel in Ramah, moreover, is not grudging with her tears. She will weep for all her children. The warehoused ones in New York City are present, then, with the baby at Bethlehem, and with the exiles in Babylon, and with the lost boy in Genesis. On the horizon of mother Rachel, all are the same, all her abused, destroyed children who must be grieved to perpetuity, "refusing to be comforted." And Kozol, in an act of courageous imagination, shows us that our policy on homelessness is indeed a "final solution," a betrayal of the beloved city, a city completely dissolved in tears. All of this might be said in a completely different way. But Kozal could not have said it another way, because the text lingers, and the sobs echo. And in a flash, this becomes that, New York becomes Jerusalem, and the grief is unrelieved. Waiting for comfort, but not yet comforted.

III

In Jer. 36, there is a most remarkable narrative account of the production of the Jeremiah scroll, which became the book of Jeremiah. Scholars have spent great energy trying to decide precisely what was in the scroll, in its several recensions. I regard all such "historical" conclusions as useless and am interested in the dramatic portrayal of the narrative itself. The scroll, through the course of this narrative, develops through the following steps.

- Jeremiah dictates to Baruch "all the words which the LORD had spoken to him."
- Baruch is sent to read the scroll in public, perhaps to evoke repentance.
- Baruch reads it in the temple, in the chamber of Gemariah, son of Shaphan.
- Baruch reads it a second time, to a second, more important layer of officials who are alarmed.
- Baruch and Jeremiah are sent into hiding, for the officials promptly recognize this is a dangerous, subversive document.
- The scroll is read before king Jehoiachim, who shreds it and "rends" the scroll. (The king, unlike the officials, is not at all alarmed).[9]
- Yahweh hides Baruch and Jeremiah.
- Jeremiah, at the behest of Yahweh, writes a second scroll, and "many similar words were added to it."

This narrative account suggests (a) Yahweh is involved in scroll making, (b) scroll making is dangerous, for it is public and challenges the monarchy,

and (c) Jeremiah the scroll maker had important public allies who understood that royal policy was foolish and self-destructive. Thus, in the end, the
conflict evoked by the scroll is between royal power and *scroll power*. The
narrative concludes with the notice that the king cannot defeat the scroll.

It is possible to judge, as scholars have, that we have here one account of
the actual way in which a biblical book came into existence. Perhaps so, if
one credits the narrative with that kind of historicity. Or it is possible to say
that this narrative chapter marks the moment of canonizing, when Israel
became "a people of the book." Indeed, there is no doubt that somewhere
in the matrix of Deuteronomy and Jeremiah circles, the book (scroll)
became authoritative, not simply as a literary activity, but as the assertion
of a certain kind of canonical, theological authority.

I do not suggest that this chapter in Jeremiah has any specific future in
which it is elsewhere quoted. But I do want to suggest that the dangerous,
bold process of bookmaking for religious authority, in which Yahweh, Jeremiah, Baruch, and the political leaders are said to be involved, is foundational for the sense of Bible as it has been operative in Western culture.

1. The primal text to which I refer, which I suggest is rooted in and linked
to Jer. 36, is the narrative of the temptation of Jesus in Matt. 4:1-13 (compare Luke 4:1-13). In that narrative, Jesus is confronted by the devil and is
tempted three times, invited each time to act in obedience to the devil, and
thereby to forsake his own vocation and identity. Each time Jesus responds
to the devil to resist the denial and to refuse obedience to the devil, he does
so with a quote from Deuteronomy (Matt. 4:4 = Deut. 8:3; Matt. 4:7 =
Deut. 6:16; Matt. 4:10 = Deut. 6:5).

Jesus is equipped with a scroll (Deuteronomy) as his only and adequate
defense against the seduction of the devil. This casting of the encounter is
not unlike the confrontation of Jer. 36, in which prophetic-covenantal faith
has only a scroll with which to oppose destructive royal power. In both
cases, the scroll is adequate. There are, of course, all kinds of dangers in this
claim, dangers of oppressive literalism and bibliolatry. These dangers, however, do not detract from the main positive point. Children of this text find
the text to be an adequate place from which to muster an alternative existence in the world, in challenge against whatever the powers may be. It is
indeed an odd claim, made by the peoples of the book, as it is not made
about any other book in any other publicly effective religious tradition.
Thus in Matt. 4 (and Luke 4), there is self-consciousness in the New Testament community that this is already a fully texted community.

This odd account of text formation portrays Yahweh as a character fully
engaged in text production. This community recognized that there is something at work here other than their own voice. There is an otherness, a surplus marked by an irresistible and savage holiness, which is uncompromising.
Thus the text in Jeremiah understands that in some inscrutable way, liberated prophetic imagination and experience take the form of a scroll.

This is an odd claim for a scroll. It is an equally odd claim for Yahweh. It is such an odd claim that José Faur has proposed that the God of the Jews, unlike Greek gods, is a maker of texts, a giver of scripture.[10] Here as in Jer. 2:6-8, much of Jewish fidelity concerns right utterance, and now the God of the Jews is also involved in the matter of right utterance.

3. Jer. 36, along with Matt. 4 (Luke 4), attests to the danger and the power of being a texted people. The prophetic tradition provides something like a scripting of reality, not in totalitarian ways, but in ways that seed and authorize an alternative imagination. This texted quality to reality suggests to me three points, which I note briefly.

(a) The texting claim of Jer. 36 relates nicely to the claim of Paul Ricoeur that all of life in its public dimension is textual. Such a claim flies in the face of an open, universal notion of reality, and tilts reality in the direction of what is local and concrete. Or put another way, it moves against what George Lindbeck terms "experiential-expressive," and toward what he calls "cultural-linguistic" understandings of reality.[11] These texts as authorizing tradition bespeak discipline, membership, and, in the end, vocation.

(b) This textual tradition, over time, has provided the endless authorization of a counterexistence in the world, a counterexistence radically exemplified in Jesus of Nazareth. Inside the Christian community, for example, it is the text that has endlessly authorized revolution, as in the cases of Augustine, Luther, and Barth. But the authorization of counterexistence is not limited to the ecclesial community, for it spills over into the public community as well. Thus we notice, for example, it was biblical cadences that authorized Martin Luther King. Michael Walzer, moreover, has chronicled the way in which the text (especially Exodus in his case) has powered various revolutions.[12] Moreover, it will not do in this context and usage to regard the Bible as a "cultural artifact" (whatever that may mean). Repeatedly and in surprising circumstance, the Bible has been an impetus, a summons, an authorization to undertake bold action, which may be revolutionary or subversive. While the powerful may reduce or diminish the Bible or, as King Jehoachim sought to do with the scroll, to eliminate it, the text keeps surfacing as a "weapon of the weak."[13]

(c) The scroll text so dramatically actualized in Jer. 36 is an utterance that keeps uttering wherever the text is made available. It is now clear that written utterance has a kind of freedom from context that spoken utterance does not. And this written utterance explodes always again in odd, energetic, and transformative ways. The simple point I wish to make here is that such texted reality is a great and relentless enemy of silence. The community of this text has learned, many times over, that enforced silence kills (compare Ps. 39:1-3).[14] All of this is evident in actual practice, without any appeal to any special theory of authority for this text. This text authorizes the mute to speak and to know what to say in the face of life-canceling power.

IV

The text concerning the "new covenant" in Jer. 31:31-34 is an exceedingly influential and important text, but also one freighted with enormous difficulty in the history of interpretation:

> The days are surely coming, says the LORD, when I will make a new covenant with the house of Israel and the house of Judah. It will not be like the covenant that I made with their ancestors when I took them by the hand to bring them out of the land of Egypt—a covenant that they broke, though I was their husband, says the LORD. But this is the covenant that I will make with the house of Israel after those days, says the LORD; I will put my law within them, and I will write it on their hearts; and I will be their God, and they shall be my people. No longer shall they teach one another, or say to each other, "Know the LORD," for they shall all know me, from the least of them to the greatest, says the LORD; for I will forgive their iniquity and remember their sin no more.

1. Israel had understood itself (from the beginning of its theological self-discernment) as the people of Sinai who stood under radical demands from Yahweh. The structure of the Sinai covenant concerned commands that carried with them rigorous sanctions of blessing and curse. This construct of life with Yahweh was given its classic articulation in Deuteronomic circles, and in various ways counted upon by the prophets—of these, none more so than the tradition of Jeremiah, shaped as it is by Deuteronomic influence (compare 11:1-8). The events of 587 and the loss of Jerusalem evoked the theological conviction in Judah that the covenant of Sinai was a spent force. The God of the command was now completely exhausted with recalcitrant Israel. As a consequence, the covenant was terminated. In light of that perceived termination, there is wholesale grief in Israel (as in the book of Lamentations) but also bewilderment about Yahweh's inclination toward the exiled community.

2. It is into this context of grief and bewilderment that there comes this extraordinary articulation of new covenant in 31:31-34. Evidently, the old covenant "that they broke" cannot be counted upon. But the *new* covenant! The term is clear. It is "new." If it is new, then there is indeed a season of discontinuity between what was old with Yahweh and what is now given. It is possible, alternatively, to take the word *new* as *renew*, to reestablish and revivify what was old. Such a rendering would assert continuity.

The text invites interpretive energy to the issue of "continuity and discontinuity."[15] Is the community of covenant now to be constituted after the break of exile the same community as heretofore? If it is the same, how new is this? And if it is new and different, then what about the old community and all its claims? It has not been possible to sort out the questions logically, so we tend to mumble, recognizing that there are present elements of both continuity and discontinuity.[16] However that is to be settled, it is clear that both the old and the new are operative in the community of Israel. What is new is new availability in Israel for the Torah, new acknowledgment of Yahweh's sovereignty, and new, radical measures of forgiveness. It is not necessary, inside the Jewish conversation, to be clearer than this.

3. The text, however, has largely been preempted by the New Testament community of Christians, as that community was separated from the synagogue. With that drastic and painful separation, it followed readily to claim that what was old and rejected was Judaism, and what was new, under the aegis of forgiveness, was the Christian community. Thus old and new were now understood, in Christian circles, in terms of discontinuity. And this claim was enhanced by the rendering of "new covenant" in the Latin as *New Testament*. This usage of the text made it easy to claim, to the satisfaction of those who claimed it, that the text had in purview exactly the Christian community that was to displace and supersede Judaism as the covenanted people of God.

Thus the text lingered in Judaism, until it exploded in Christianity to serve a wholly new purpose, namely "supersessionism," whereby it was claimed that Christianity had superseded Judaism.[17] The New Testament as a whole does not everywhere claim supersessionism, as is evident in Romans 9–11. It is equally clear, however, that there are indeed supersessionist texts that are unambiguous. This is especially the case in Hebrews, which quotes our Jeremiah text in 8:8-13 and 11:16-17. The writer can conclude, moreover:

> In speaking of a "new covenant," he has made the first one obsolete. And what is obsolete and growing old will soon disappear.
> (8:13)

This is, in retrospect, a staggering and scandalous claim. Considered hermeneutically, what happens in this text is what characteristically happens in the interpretive reuse of text. Texts take on meanings not present in the original presentation of the text. Thus, in making its large claim for Jesus, the writer of Hebrews has this text lingering from Jeremiah, ready at hand. And now the text is uttered with new, revolutionary (and offensive!) force.

From that reuse of the text, moreover, Christianity has long practiced supersessionism that not only enhanced the claims of the Christian Gospel, but derogated Judaism.[18] What we see in this textual reuse is a text of Judaism that is now turned as a text against Judaism. Anti-Semitism, which culminates in the Shoah, surely has many and complex causes. But there is no doubt that theological supersessionism, given its clearest expression in this reused text, figures behind that sordid history. Steven Katz has shown how such supersessionism, while not to be blamed for the Holocaust, helped to generate the circumstances for it, by imagining "the Jews" as an odd, ideological category.[19]

4. This "new covenant" now claimed for Christianity has become an intensely theological-christological claim, as in 1 Cor. 11:25. It is also the case, however, that the category of "covenant/new covenant" entered into the political vocabulary and political theory of the West, largely through the Calvinist tradition and more especially through the work of Theodore Beza.[20] Thus "new covenant" came to be understood as a social compact between the governed and the governors, or between the strong and the weak, in order to create a viable polity with equitable social institutions and policies. While the move from an Old Testament text into modern political theory and practice is a complex one, there is no doubt that the "ideology" of covenant has been instrumental in shaping Western society. For the actual function of this notion of polity, reference may be made to *The Broken Covenant* by Robert Bellah, and in a curious way to *The Covenant* by James Michener, who considers the Dutch Reformed theology that shaped South Africa, and even the tentative probe of President Clinton into "the politics of the new covenant."[21] Seen as a source of new polity, "the new covenant" is not a proposal for individualism, as Jer. 31:33 is often taken to be. Rather, it is in fact a powerful protest against the individualist autonomy of modernity, and an insistence that we are indeed members one of another.

5. The text lingers. It is not at all clear how a covenantal polity will reemerge in the midst of a widespread and uncritical commoditization in Western culture. In the meantime, however, the text of 31:31-34 has resurfaced in another, happy way. Western Christianity has had to face its long and unhappy story of supersessionism, which has lived at the edge of anti-Semitism. Under the impetus of the Second Vatican Council, the pope, finally, has pursued a theological rapprochement with Judaism under the rubric "The Covenant Never Revoked."[22] The covenant to which reference is made is God's covenant with Judaism. And the phrase "never revoked" directly and intentionally contradicts the ancient claims of supersessionism. Thus Vatican theology has moved, albeit belatedly, in the direction of recognizing that Yahweh's commitment to the Jewish community is an enduring one, so that the new/renewed covenant of 31:31-34 is of course with God's people, the Jewish people. In this context, appeal is made to the phrasing "everlasting covenant," a phrase that became especially important in the exile at the brink of rejection (compare Gen. 9:16; Ezek. 37:26).[23] There are of course difficult theological issues yet to be thought through, given exclusivist Christian claims. While that work remains, it is clear that this long-lingering text has exploded in yet a fresh way, to overcome "a strong misreading" (in Hebrews) that now strikes even a Christian theological reader as a disastrous misreading.

V

At the conclusion of Jeremiah—as it is arranged in the Greek (Christian) order—there is a series of "Oracles against the Nations," a standard prophetic genre. The oracles against the nations occur as a special corpus in many of the prophetic books.[24] They are a stylized way in which prophetic faith asserts Yahweh's governance over non-Israelite nations and over the international power process. In every case, moreover, the nation named is identified negatively as one that has violated Yahweh's purpose, and who must therefore be punished. While the genre has a focused theological intention, it also has the force of deabsolutizing every self-aggrandizing political power.

This collection of such oracles in Jeremiah (46–51) begins with an oracle against Egypt (46) and concludes with a long oracle against Babylon (50–51).[25] This latter oracle is important to Jeremiah, both because it stands in the final position in the book and seems to make the climactic statement of the book in its final form, and because Jeremiah is pervasively positive toward Babylon. Here, however, the field is reversed. The empire that had been seen as a tool of Yahweh to whom Judah should yield is now exposed as Yahweh's enemy, whom Yahweh must finally crush. In the book of Jeremiah, Babylon is Yahweh's short-term ally. But because of its imperious self-interest, Babylon in the long run can be nothing other than Yahweh's adversary, who will in the end be defeated and destroyed by Yahweh.

Because the oracle against Babylon, like every such oracle in the genre, has historical specificity in its reference to Babylon, it is not easy to see how or in what way this oracle could be reused. The oracle clearly applies to the Babylonian empire in the sixth century, and that empire no longer exists. Thus the subject of the oracle has evaporated.

Here as much as anywhere, it is important to move beyond historical reference in our consideration of a prophetic text. What evidently has happened is that the text, in its enduring canonical function, has lost its concrete historical perspective that it once had. As an enduring, canonical text, it no longer cares about or addresses a sixth-century empire. In fact, "Babylon" has become a cipher to refer to any and every brutalizing superpower. And "Nebuchadnezzar," as in Daniel, has become a metaphorical reference to every exploitative, self-aggrandizing superpower on the world stage. A later reader of the text, who lives and imagines outside a sixth-century context, inevitably and intuitively makes this move beyond historical specificity. Thus the tradition references Babylon. But the reexperiencing of the text depends upon moving beyond Babylon to some other, subsequent historical reference, one that belongs to the imaginative world of the reader's own experience, and not at all to the horizon of the first reference.

In order to have a feel for the power and intention of the text, I have selected representative verses, but even these of necessity must be rather extensive. The oracle begins with an ostensive victory announcement, a messenger announcing the good news that hated Babylon has fallen:

> Declare among the nations and proclaim,
>> set up a banner and proclaim,
>> do not conceal it, say:
> Babylon is taken,
>> Bel is put to shame,
>> Merodach is dismayed.
> Her images are put to shame,
>> her idols are dismayed. (Jer. 50:2)

Babylon falls, because its arrogance has evoked the enmity of Yahweh, who declares war on Babylon:

> I am against you, O arrogant one,
>> says the Lord GOD of hosts;
> for your time has come,
>> the time when I will punish you.
> The arrogant one shall stumble and fall,
>> with no one to raise him up,
> and I will kindle a fire in his cities,
>> and it will devour everything around him. (vv. 31-32)

The result is that Nebuchadnezzar, the awesome king of Babylon, is as helpless and distressed as a woman in labor:

> The king of Babylon heard news of them,
>> and his hands fell helpless;
> anguish seized him,
>> pain like that of a woman in labor. (v. 43)

Indeed, the macho world of the imperial army is mocked in a roundly sexist way. These would-be soldiers have "become women":

> The warriors of Babylon have given up fighting,
>> they remain in their strongholds;
> their strength has failed,
>> they have become women;
> her buildings are set on fire,
>> her bars are broken. (51:30)

They offer no resistance, so that their invaders may do what they want at will. And now the poem describes the assault. It is Yahweh who invades.

But "a destroyer" has come up against Babylon. In the first instant, we imagine the destroyer to be Cyrus the Persian, who is not mentioned:

> Listen!—a cry from Babylon!
> A great crashing from the land of the Chaldeans!

> For the LORD is laying Babylon waste,
>   and stilling her loud clamor.
> Their waves roar like mighty waters,
>   the sound of their clamor resounds;
> for a destroyer has come against her,
>   against Babylon;
> her warriors are taken,
>   their bows are broken;
> for the LORD is a God of recompense,
>   he will repay in full.
> I will make her officials and her sages drunk,
>   also her governors, her deputies, and her warriors;
> they shall sleep a perpetual sleep and never awake,
>   says the King, whose name is the LORD of hosts. (51:54-57)

Nothing is left of Babylon, nothing but burned gates, level land, exhaustion. All is spent and then fire. The course of the poetry is a process whereby the subsequent hearer of the text is made to live through and experience the startling progress of the destruction. It is clearly inadequate to reflect on the oracle historically. The poetry works primarily to generate affect, so that the hearer of the text can imaginatively picture or enact the fall of the mighty, who cannot finally stand against Yahweh.

In 50:35-38 we are offered an extraordinary piece of rhetoric. One notices the repetitious, irresistible hammering of the destructive force in the speech. The utterance utilizes no verbs. The action is too abrupt, the assault is too quick. The articulation is too terse for full grammar:

> Sword against the Chaldeans, says the LORD,
>   and against the inhabitants of Babylon,
>   and against her officials and her sages!
> A sword against the diviners,
>   so that they may become fools!
> A sword against her warriors,
>   so that they may be destroyed!
> A sword against her horses and against her chariots,
>   and against all the foreign troops in her midst,
>   so that they may become women!
> A sword against all her treasures,
>   that they may be plundered!
> A drought against her waters,
>   that they may be dried up!
> For it is a land of images,
>   and they go mad over idols. (vv. 35-38)

Thus ever to tyrants!

This prophetic utterance generates for us a very particular, much hated, deeply scorned Babylon. The text persists, no doubt, because all that is assigned to Babylon with such force and passion can as well be reassigned to other brutal powers, which also need to be hated, scorned, defeated, and finally destroyed. The poem offers a mood and propensity about which every subjugated people knows. It ponders the seeming omnipotence of the oppressor, but it also imagines in hateful hope, fueled by resentment and faith, the painful demise of the oppressor. Thus the poet offers us not a lesson in history, but a usable cipher that gives access to suffering and hope on large scale.

2. The book of Revelation, in the New Testament, takes up the cipher of Babylon, offered to us in this oracle from Jeremiah:[26]

> Fallen, fallen is Babylon the great!
>> It has become a dwelling place of demons,
> a haunt of every foul and hateful bird,
>> a haunt of every foul and hateful beast . . .
> Alas, alas, the great city,
>> clothed in fine linen,
>>> in purple and scarlet,
>> with jewels, and with pearls!
> For in one hour all this wealth has been laid waste! . . .
> With such violence Babylon the great city
>> will be thrown down,
>> and will be found no more . . . (Rev. 18:2,16-17a, 21b)

Clearly the text is not concerned with Babylon now long gone. In this profoundly suggestive literature, Babylon has resurfaced, now in the form of hated, brutalizing Rome. The text has no need to decode or interpret for its primary readers. They know, for they live in the world of this brutalization. They participate readily and easily in the poison and the hope and the gloating that this literature voices and legitimates. It would not occur to these hearers that "Babylon" ever referred to an ancient sixth-century empire, for the reference is clearly, as it always is, here and now, here and now with suffering, here and now with buoyant, confident hope. Babylon, this one or any one, cannot survive the onslaught of this God, "for mighty is the Lord God who judges her" (Rev. 18:8).

3. The cipher Babylon was kept prepared and waiting for subsequent use. And therefore it was ready when Martin Luther reached for words and images with which to voice his devastating critique of the Roman Church and its sacramental system. So he wrote, in 1520, "The Babylonian Captivity of the Church."[27] He found in his own context the power of the gospel to be completely controlled and domesticated by the impervious indifference and brutality of the Roman hierarchy. And of course, he was able thereby to suggest to his cohorts in the Reformation that they were God's

faithful remnant, laboring against great odds, exactly like little Judah, sure to prevail. Luther had to explain to none of his hearers what he meant. The imaginative maneuver from then to now, from there to here, was inescapable. The cipher worked, and it brought with it not only its powerful theological force, but also its irresistible rhetorical power that spilled over into political decisions. The theological force always comes with rhetorical power, because the prophetic tradition that becomes prophetic reexperience is always an act of concrete, generative rhetoric.

4. Among the uses of this oracle-generated cipher of Babylon, we ask finally about its contemporary usage, as we ponder the world of superpowers. No doubt somewhere, some restless, seething poet imagined the Soviet Union to be the "Whore Babylon," bound for defeat.

What I can cite is the study of Philip Wheaton and Duane Shank, whose concern is the sociopolitical viability of Central America, in the shadow of the "Colossus of the North."[28] In their study, they label the United States, the last great, exploitative superpower, as Babylon. Babylon in power, Babylon in exploitative indifference, and Babylon sure to fall. The Babylon connection is always on the lips of the little community, against the colossus.

But the rhetoric is not just about "good us" and "bad them." It is also about the inscrutable power of God, who "brings low and also exalts" (1 Sam. 2:7). It asserts a "wild card" in the power process that deabsolutizes all claims to power and all postures of stability. And the way of this wild card, the prophetic tradition suggests, is not militarism, but rhetoric, a key instrument in the fall as in the rise.

5. It is abundantly clear that the horizon of the prophetic tradition is not just *Israel* and not just *justice for widows and orphans*. Rather, the horizon is *Yahweh's governance*. It is equally clear that in the world of modernity, such claims have largely disappeared from the lips of those who claim this text. The loss of this public rhetoric is an enormously costly loss, because it means the withdrawal of biblical imagination from the most urgent spheres of our common life.

The cipher of Babylon, I propose, raises the issue of whether such rhetoric is at all available for public life amid the cynical reductionism of modernity. Perhaps it is, but only among the marginalized who have no other leverage except rhetoric and imagination. It occurs to me that a modern, secular form of this rhetoric of limit may be found in Paul Kennedy's fine book, *The Rise and Fall of the Great Powers*.[29] Kennedy opines that a combination of population, territory, and natural resources produces a limit for any political power, or any superpower, beyond which a power or superpower will self-destruct by overextension. Kennedy makes no explicit moral claim and shuns all rhetoric that could suggest such. But Kennedy's argument about the rise and fall of the Dutch empire, and the rise and fall of the British empire, and the putative rise and fall of the U.S. empire, is that there are limits that must be honored in self-restraint. The alternative, the inevitable alternative to self-restraint, is self-destruction.

Kennedy would not express the matter as I have. But I have wondered if his argument is not parallel to the startling, enigmatic rhetoric of the prophetic tradition. In the purview of Kennedy, one may suggest that the recovery and reuse of this rhetoric may be urgent in the midst of the last superpower, which is endlessly tempted beyond self-restraint to self-destruction.

VI

Three conclusions:

1. The reexperiencing of the prophetic tradition—that is, the rehearing and respeaking of the texts with fresh contemporaneity—does not depend primarily upon critical and technical interpretive matters, but upon a capacity for imagination and intuition, coupled with courage, which dares to assert that these texts, concretely located and specifically addressed, can now be and must be concretely relocated and specifically readdressed as illuminating and revelatory in contemporary contexts. Those who are able to make this stunning interpretive maneuver are those who can give themselves over to the text and its startling, enigmatic quality without encumbrance. One cannot anticipate the emergence of such voices when they are nurtured and evoked in the community of the text, but only recognize and receive them with gratitude when they emerge. They are the ones who permit the explosions of text whereby the world is transformed.

2. But to recognize and celebrate the value of the explosive agents who emerge in the community of the text is not to denigrate the work of scribes who preserve the text.[30] It is the work of scribes to assure the lingering, to keep the text available, to secure the text, and to surround the text with the best interpretive possibilities that can be ventured. When "prophecy ends," scribes guard the text that results from prophetic utterance. They do so, even if unwittingly, in order to preserve the text until another prophet comes, who will be grasped by the lingering text, and who becomes the occasion for a fresh textual explosion. Thus the work of *lingering* and the work of *explosion* are in tandem. It remains clear that the lingerers (sometimes malingerers) make possible the prophetic respeakers yet to come.

3. Finally, I want to comment upon the urgency of this reexperiencing of the prophetic tradition. I do so by reference to the study of Martin Heidegger by John Caputo, *Demythologizing Heidegger*.[31] Caputo concludes that Heideggers's fascination with Nazi ideology was not an odd, peculiar interest, but the natural and inevitable outcome of his philosophical, totalizing universalism. Against Heidegger, Caputo opposes what he calls the "prophetic imagination" of Emmanuel Levinas, Jacques Derrida, and Jean-François

Lyotard. The contrast that Caputo proposes is stunning in its power and in its pertinence for our discussion. Caputo opposes to Heidegger (a) Derrida's "Undeconstructability of Justice," and (b) Levinas's "Hyperbolic Justice."[32] Of these formidable Jewish interpreters, who reexperience the prophetic tradition, Caputo writes:

> I want at this point to identity this jewgreek imagination, this myth of justice, this prophetic or quasi-prophetic call for justice, for justice as mercy and compassion, issuing in particular from Derrida and Levinas in order precisely to reinstate what has been so radically excluded by the myth of Being.[33]

Of Levinas, Caputo writes:

> The work of Levinas comes over us today like the voice of a Jewish prophet, like the cry of Amos demanding that justice flow over the land like water, like a prophet among the postmodernists, inspiring a prophetic postmodernism.[34]

Of Derrida, he writes:

> But then is Derrida's undeconstructible justice prophetic justice? Is Derrida the latest in a long line of Jewish prophets? That would be mad, excessive, too much, too scandalous, too emphatic, an overemphasis, and he has warned us against such exaggerations . . . but I would say what Derrida has said, that this discourse on undeconstructible justice is "not far away" from prophetic discourse.[35]

And then this:

> The voice of the prophet interrupts the self-assured voices of the powerful, of the arche, the princes of this world, bringing them up short, calling them to account for themselves. That is why the prophets had a habit of getting themselves killed, a most serious occupational hazard. They were perhaps a little mad, mad for justice, mad about injustice, and maybe, just a little, plain mad.[36]

The prophetic tradition preserves for us these staggering enactments of redemptive madness. The madness lingers in and through the text. That is why the text has been kept until now. When the text is resurfaced, revoiced, reuttered, reexperienced, it sometimes turns out to be the only sanity in town.

2   Rereading the Book of Isaiah

IN HIS RICH AND SUGGESTIVE STUDIES OF THE HISTORY OF MODERN CRITI-
cism, John Rogerson has traced the primary intellectual and theological
currents that have shaped our study. These include rationalism, pietism,
and orthodoxy. Along with tracing these complex currents, Rogerson has
inevitably cited specific instances and cases of the ways in which emerging
criticism has shaped our understanding of the texts. Among others, he has
exhibited the way in which the unity and single authorship of Isaiah has
been critically undermined, until we have arrived at a critical consensus
concerning the tripartite structure of the book of Isaiah and the role of the
so-called Servant Songs in interpretation.

Because Rogerson's research has not reached into the later twentieth century in any sustained way, his report on critical developments in the book
of Isaiah does not reach as far as the recent discussion of "canonical" Isaiah. A number of scholars, but especially Brevard Childs and Ronald
Clements, have been preoccupied with showing how the critically divided
book of Isaiah can be understood with canonical coherence.[1] Indeed, scholarly work on the book of Isaiah at the present time concerns the tension and
relatedness between the established critical consensus and emerging attention to canonical claims.

The subject of this collection, "The Bible in Human Society," however,
sets our thinking in a quite different direction. The phrase "in human
society" considers the Bible not as an object of considered reflective
scholarship, but rather as the use of texts in an intentional but not critically knowing way. Such use of texts may or may not be informed by
scholarly opinion, but it tends to use specific texts in life contexts, without attention to either critical consensus or canonical shape. Such texts
are regularly taken up seriatim and freshly situated in quite different
interpretive occasions, so that the text claims for itself new meanings.[2]

Here I will identify and consider briefly five such uses. I refer to these as
"strong rereadings." Readers will recognize my allusion to Harold Bloom's
notion of "strong misreadings."[3] By the phrase, Bloom, as I understand
him, did not mean "wrong" readings, but only courageous acts of interpretation that read texts in new directions without subservience to any established or even "clear" meaning. I use the term "reread" to refer to what
Bloom intends, but also to suggest that the new readings, given the readers'
situations, offer credible readings.

I do not suggest that such ad hoc readings, which may violate critical
consensus or canonical intentionality, constitute any correction of or

protest against more "normative" readings. But they may give us pause. They may give us pause because the more biblical texts are utilized "in human society" the less the texts are under scholarly or "canonical" constraints. If or when the use of the Bible is no longer "in human society" but only in scholarship, we shall have arrived, I suspect, at a situation when the text no longer functions with vitality. Its vitality is at the same time a measure of its public use and of the limits of scholarly or "canonical" restraints. Such a phenomenon may give us pause when we ponder the fact that the scholarly and "canonical" enterprises do not in any comprehensive way inform readings that are serious, even if divergent.

1

The first text I cite is an early text of Martin Luther. Early in his move toward his settled "Reformation" convictions, Luther participated in a "Heidelberg Dispute" on April 26, 1518, in which he first articulated his definitive "Theology of the Cross."[4] In his argument presented at the disputation, he offered forty theses, for which he then offered "proofs." From that debate conducted in the community of the Augustinians in Heidelberg, I will cite three theses of Luther:

> 19. That person does not deserve to be called a theologian who looks upon the invisible things of God as though they were clearly perceptible in those things which have actually happened (Rom. 1:20).
> 20. He deserves to be called a theologian, however, who comprehends the visible and manifest things of God seen through suffering and the cross.
> 21. A theology of glory calls evil good and good evil. A theology of the cross calls the thing what it actually is.[5]

I cite theses 19 and 20 because in these central claims Luther enunciates his conviction that the "invisible things of God" are indeed hidden and not "clearly perceptible" and that the "manifest and visible things of God" are seen through "suffering and the cross."[6] In these claims, Luther's "theology of the cross" moves radically against "reason" to depend upon *revelation* and against "glory" to *suffering* as the medium and measure of God's disclosure.

But it is thesis 21 that directly concerns us. Luther here continues the sharp and dramatic antithesis in which he has begun, contrasting glory/cross, strength/weakness, wisdom/folly, good/evil. Our direct interest is that the thesis itself is an unacknowledged reference to Isa. 5:20:

> Ah, you who call evil good and good evil,
>> who put darkness for light and light for darkness,
>> who put bitter for sweet and sweet for bitter!

In his commentary, where he is more disciplined and attentive to the text, Luther takes this "woe" to refer to the "pestilent teachers."[7] "They blaspheme and rail at it (the Word of God) but proclaim their own ungodly ideas and wisdom of the flesh, things which are never good."[8] In his commentary, Luther draws the series of woe sayings away from the practical ordering of life to theological teaching. In his Heidelberg theses, however, he goes much further. Now the simple contrast between "good and evil" is drawn into Luther's programmatic contrast of "glory and cross," the former being the way of the world, the latter the demanding, scandalous way of the gospel. Thus calling things by their right names is not simply faithful discernment, as an Israelite sage might have taught, but it is the submission of all discernment to the singular rule of the cross.[9]

Luther demonstrates how a particular text is by theological conviction profoundly transposed to serve an "evangelical" program. This is not to say that Luther takes the text away from Isaiah, but that he requires a rereading of Isaiah as "a theologian of the cross." The series of woes in Isa. 5:8-22 and 10:1-4 now become conclusions drawn about the hiddenness of God (on which, see Isa. 45:15), and the judgment that the discerning eye of "natural man," that is, those not under the suffering of the cross, cannot see clearly at all. Except for the crucial nature of the cross (a big exception!), this is not so far removed from Isaiah's apparent claim that the kings in Jerusalem, without faith, do not see and do not trust what God is doing in their common life.

II

At the very beginning of his publishing career, Karl Marx wrote polemical comments on political items in the *Rheinische Zeitung*.[10] On October 25, 1842, he responded to an action of the Diet of the Rhineland, which prohibited stealing firewood from enclosed land.[11] The practice of the peasants was roundly condemned by the Diet, which was of course composed of property owners who enclosed land and who granted the poor no right to take much needed wood from their property.

The one-sided and predictable action of the Diet provided an early occasion for Marx in his critique of private property and in his analysis of the law as a tool of private property. In his analysis, Marx considers the way in which an economy dominated by the propertied is separated from the realities of the social fabric in ways that are inevitably destructive.

In addition to his critique of private property and partisan law, which remained constant in his social analysis, Marx explicated a practical understanding of the poor who need wood in order to survive, and who must violate "law" in order to have wood. Marx asks, on what grounds are they authorized to steal? His answer is, on the basis of the law or right of "custom." That is, there are old, well-established social practices, long before the imposed laws of private property, which were accepted as legitimating the gathering of wood on open land. Marx's positive concern is to show that this "law of custom" is still valid, is still "grounded in reason," and is the customary "right of poverty" for those who have no other recourse. Moreover, he insists that this ancient and time-honored practice belongs to the "rightful nature of things," because nonowners have rights, that is, protection accorded to the powerless.[12]

In the very life and conduct of the propertyless class, one can see a correlation between nature and poverty, which creates a livable order that cannot be violated because it is manifestly human.[13] Against the "control of the propertyless," Marx juxtaposes "the justice of the poor." In his second major move, Marx argues that this natural right has become in fact the "law of the state," which the Diet is not free to contradict. Thus, in what strikes one as the reification of the state, Marx takes the true and proper function of the state as something more elemental and ultimate that these propertied lawmakers cannot change when they vote merely by their own interests.

This peculiar, but characteristic, analysis of Marx brings us to the specific point of our concern. In a climactic judgment against the Diet, Marx contrasts the true concerns of the state with the frivolous and illegitimate actions of the Diet:

> Deine Wege sind nicht meine Wege,
> und deine Gedanken sind nicht meine Gedanken![14]
>
> (Your ways are not my ways,
> and your thoughts are not my thoughts.)

It is a common interpretive judgment that these words in Isa. 55:8 are addressed to Jewish exiles in Babylon, asserting that repentance is the way out of exile. Informed by the study of Norman Gottwald, I have recently suggested that this assertion is a summons to embrace an intentional Jewish identity and to resist "assimilation" into the ideology of Babylonian power and Babylonian religious legitimacy.[15]

Marx of course has no interest in such historicizing. As a polemicist, he brings the text to his own urgent argument and uses what must have been powerful religious rhetoric (without acknowledging his citation of the text) to form an absolute contrast between two thoughts and two ways. The contrast is between the legitimation of what Nicholas Lash terms "reprobate materialists" and the natural right of the poor, which is the law of the state. Marx will not, of course, identify this alternative way (of the state) with the "way of Yahweh," for his opponents have already preempted theological legitimacy. The alternative way is rooted in the reality of the society, based upon reason, a mandate entrusted to the state. Thus the true state stands as a counter to this Rhineland Diet, which violates right and reason and disobeys the true mandate of the state. As in the words of Isa. 55 against Babylon, Marx intends to legitimate those who have interests, thoughts, ways, and intentions of their own that violate this "more excellent way."

Arnold van Leeuwen regards Marx's use of Isa. 55:8 as altogether appropriate to the argument and not tacked on. He observes that "the spirit of the Torah" is palpably evident throughout this article.[16] Thus we have a powerful rereading in Isaiah that turns the text against those who imagine they enjoy theological legitimacy for their own interests.

Three comments by way of extrapolation from Marx occur to me. First, E. P. Thompson has analyzed in some detail the practice of plebeian discourse and activity in eighteenth-century England.[17] He notes, as Marx did, that the dominant socioeconomic forces have established social hegemony and that the peasants have no court of appeal beyond "custom." Thompson comments on "the interface between, on the one hand, law and ruling ideologies, and, on the other, common right usages and customary consciousness."[18] Thompson concludes that the older custom constitutes "a moral economy," which was in profound conflict with the new "political economy."[19] It is "moral" for the same reason Marx gives. And though Thompson concludes with no such scriptural reference, his argument for England closely parallels that of Marx on the Rhineland situation.

Second, in his programmatic study of economic history, Karl Polyani probes the enclosure laws of Speenhamland in eighteenth-century England, whereby the old peasant right of land use began to be legally prohibited.[20] Thus Marx's argument does not concern a specific Diet action only, but a massive, systematic shift of people and land that haunts the modern world. The practice of enclosure, now legally justified, prepares the way for modern, rapacious individualism.

Third, the argument of Marx is not far distant from the programmatic notion of God's "preferential option for the poor," a programmatic phrase current in the Latin America church. Of course such liberation theology is often dismissed as too much indebted to Marx. It is worth noticing that Marx's argument is a substantive one and not simply a rhetorical flourish. The sum of the argument is that, as Isa. 55 asserts, there is more to which folk are summoned than the benefit of immediate advantage given through hegemonic control. Marx manages to make such a critical theological claim without "naming the name." Nonetheless, the words of Isaiah continue to haunt the entire social settlement upon which he reflects and which now becomes increasingly void of credibility.

III

The emergence of a "feminist" hermeneutic has caused a new kind of attention to the text that raises issues related to sexual imagery and metaphor.[21]

A variety of texts have been found to be pertinent to the problem of patriarchal imagery and to less exclusivist alternatives. The text that I consider, though others might be cited, is Isa. 49:15-16:

> Can a woman forget her nursing child,
>> or show no compassion for the child of her womb?
> Even these may forget,
>> yet I will not forget you.
> See, I have inscribed you on the palms of my hands;
>> your walls are continually before me.

These verses are preceded by two verses that provide a literary setting for them. In v. 13, the poet has a characteristic summons to praise, in recognition of a newness for Israel wrought by Yahweh. The reason for praise is given in the last two clauses, utilizing the term "comfort" (*nḥm*) and the verb "have compassion" (*rḥm*). This verse, however, is followed by the quotation of a communal lament, governed by the negating verbs "forsake" (*'zv*) and "forget" (*šḥk*). The stylized complaint seems to echo Lam. 5:20 and was perhaps recited regularly in exile. Its function here appears to be to reject the announcement of v. 13 and to insist upon the unrelieved exilic situation of abandonment.

In vv. 15-16, as is characteristic in Israel's liturgical texts, the complaint of v. 14 receives a response in the form of a divine utterance. The oracle intends to overcome the complaint and to provide sure ground for the credibility of the assertion of v. 13. It has much interested feminist readers that in order to provide ground for the assurance, the poet must resort to maternal imagery. Here God is said to be a "mother." It is characteristic of mothers that they do not forget a suckling child, or fail to "show compassion" for an infant who is their own. Of course they do not! But in an extreme case, they might! The mother who might forget and not show compassion is presented in the verses as a foil for Yahweh, who is a mother who transcends the conventional mother, who will never forget or fail to show compassion. The imagery of "mother God" is powerful and subtle. In order to make sense of the imagery, the "mother God" must be *like* every mother. The imagery has power because this mother God is *unlike* other mothers, for this mother God is absolute and without exception in remembering and caring for the beloved child Israel. The metaphor functions to witness to Yahweh's bottomless fidelity, even to an exiled Israel, which imagines itself to be forgotten and forsaken.

So much is a common reading of the Isaiah texts. We may, however, notice three dimensions of feminist reading that have intensified and deepened our discernment of this text. First, early in the articulation of a feminist hermeneutic, Phyllis Trible explored, with particular attention, the uses of the term *rḥm* ("womb") in the Old Testament/Hebrew Scriptures.[22] In our text, Trible observed that the term "compassion" (*rḥm*) in vv. 13, 15, and 16 makes a connection between "womb" and "compassion," and so articulates a new presence of Yahweh among the Israelites. Following Trible, this linkage has now become commonplace. But we must recognize that it was precisely the posing of a feminist question, that is, an inquiry about sexual imagery and intentionality, that evokes awareness of the rhetorical connection. Trible has daringly called attention to the "bodily reality" of Yahweh, who acts in a "womb-like" way toward beloved children who can never be forgotten.

Second, my former student Linda Chenowith one day in class, without excessive critical awareness but with great attentiveness to feminist issues, helped me see this text differently. She observed that if the child of v. 15 is a "suckling," the nursing mother must nurse, or she will experience the pain of a full breast left unsuckled.[23] That is, the mother remembers and shows "compassion" because the mother needs the child to suckle. Thus the binding of mother and child, in the metaphor, is a bodily one giving us another dimension of bodily reality, which Trible had already seen in *rḥm*.

Third, Mayer I. Gruber has taken feminist concern in a different direction.[24] He observes that 2 Isaiah is especially drawn to mother images for God, and he cites 42:14, 45:10, and 66:13 as well as other verses. Gruber is attentive to the contrast made here between mothers who forget and Yahweh who never forgets: "The Lord, who is the Mother of Israel, is not like these wicked mothers but like the good mothers."[25] Gruber's final observation, however, moves away from the intensity of the image to suggest that appeal to a mother God is a radical appeal against idolatry. He concludes:

> The lesson would seem to be that a religion which seeks to convey the Teaching of God who is above and beyond both sexes cannot succeed in conveying that Teaching if it seeks to do so in a manner which implies that a positive-divine value is attached to only the one of the two sexes.[26]

Now it may be that the general intention of these observations is transparent enough in these verses, under the general rubric of "radical fidelity." If, however, we seek to go below the concept to the symbol, we must admit that the specificity and density of this particular articulation of the fidelity on God's part is uncovered for us by feminist ways of reading.[27] What feminist readers have done is to set this text in a metanarrative of feminism that is attentive to the use of images that subvert ideology and enter into density of the metaphor mostly missed in conventional reading. The notice of the "bodily" here makes us attentive to Yahweh's active, pained engagement with the child, Israel. Yahweh's stance thus is not only one of generosity or charity, but Yahweh is indeed at risk. It is then possible to return the text to the metanarrative of scripture (and so away from any feminist metanarrative), but our reading will have been decisively transformed in the process of rereading.

Finally, we may mention the remarkable reading of this text by Mary
Gordon. Whereas current feminist reading has stressed that in this text God
is *like* a mother, only more so, in her novel *Men and Angels,* Gordon
exploits the text to establish that mothers, *unlike* God, are quite unreliable.[28] The novel tells a tale of a series of persons, each of whom had an
unreliable, if not destructive, mother. This includes Anne's mother,
Stephen's mother, Michael's mother, and especially Laura's mother. Indeed,
Laura, because of a failed family, had been driven to religion, to trust in
God who is so unlike mother. Twice, Laura refers explicitly to our passage.[29] Out of this verse, she becomes an alienated, driven, almost demonic
person, and in the end self-destructs.

The story is saturated with perplexed or hostile comments about mothers.
Thus Jane comments:

> Mother love. I haven't the vaguest idea what it means. All these
> children claiming their mothers didn't love them, and all these
> mothers saying they'd die for their children. Even women who
> beat their children say they love them, they can't live without
> them, they wouldn't dream of giving them up. "What does it
> mean 'I love my child'?"[30]

Anne and Adrian have this conversation about Laura:

> ADRIAN: What happened to her?
>
> ANNE: I don't know exactly, but I just feel it. She seems so unloved,
> so unmothered. So tremendously unhappy.
>
> ADRIAN: It's not your responsibility to make her happy.
>
> ANNE: But she lives in my house. She takes care of my children. And
> if I *can* make her happy, I should try.
>
> ADRIAN: What makes you think you can?
>
> ANNE: I don't know. Vanity, maybe.
>
> ADRIAN: Listen, you're not her mother. You're her employer. Your
> responsibility is to pay her a fair wage and not to overwork her. You
> don't have to save her life . . . You don't have to take in strays.[31]

In the end, Anne and Jane draw the conversation back to the text of Isaiah:

> ANNE (*of Laura's mother*): That woman had said she had hated
> her daughter since the moment she was born. Anne thought of
> holding her babies, of her cheeks against their cheeks, their
> mouths on her breast. The woman was a monster. Motherhood
> was a place where hate could not enter. That was what you said,

holding your baby: No one will hurt you, I will keep you from the terrible world. But that woman had brought hate with her, put a knife between her breasts, pierced her child's flesh and poured in poison.[32]

JANE: Of course it is never enough, the love of God. It is always insufficient for the human heart. It can't keep us from despair as well as the most ordinary kindness from a stranger. The love of God means nothing to a heart that is starved of human love.[33]

I cite Gordon's novel to indicate the broad range of interpretive possibilities in the text of Isaiah. Gordon has not evaded or distorted the text, but has read it from another experience, with a quite different accent. She has stayed in the field of the poem, facing the terrible issue of God being *like* and *unlike,* but finally seeing that if not loved by those we see, being loved by one we do not see is most problematic (1 John 4:20).

IV

The poem of Isa. 65:17-25 is among the most sweeping and remarkable promissory oracles of the Old Testament. Paul D. Hanson and Otto Plöger have suggested that it is the voice of expectant Judaism in its period of rehabilitation after the exile that protests against a narrow, fearful Judaism.[34] This text of course has often been taken out of the narrative of Judaism and situated in other narratives. I cite one poignant case of such rereading.

In the Canadian province of Manitoba, there was widespread labor unrest culminating in the General Strike of 1919.[35] At issue in the building and metal trades were matters of collective bargaining, better wages, and lamentable working conditions. Increasing pressure was mounted about these issues through a labor movement organized as the Winnipeg Traders and Labor Council. The labor movement in western Canada was constituted in part by the import of British Socialism and included some romanticism and an influential strand of Christian militarism.

On May 15, 1919, a strike called by the Traders and Labor Council prompted thirty thousand workers to leave their jobs. The strikers were opposed by the "Citizens Committee of 1000," composed of the moneyed power structure, which charged that the strike was instigated by Bolshevists and which undertook a campaign to resist any conciliation.

Our particular concern in this social emergency is the role played by James Shaver Woodsworth.[36] He had been a Christian pastor but had left his pastorate to become directly and actively involved with the labor issues and the possibility of socialist resolutions to the political conflict and its underlying economic causes. At the pivot point of the strike, Woodsworth, among several other prominent leaders, was arrested in a vigorous police assault. Three charges of seditious libel were brought against Woodsworth. The second was:

> That J. S. Woodsworth in or about the month of June in the year of our Lord One Thousand and Nine Hundred and Nineteen at the City of Winnipeg, in the Province of Manitoba, unlawfully and seditiously published libels in the words and figures following:
>
> Woe unto them that decree unrighteous decrees, and that write grievousness which they have prescribed, to turn aside the needy from judgment, and to take away the right from the poor of my people that widows may be their prey and that they may rob the fatherless.
>
> And they shall build houses and inhabit them, and they shall plant vineyards, and eat the fruit of them. They shall not build and another inhabit; they shall not plant and another eat, for as the days of a tree are the days of my people, and mine elect shall long enjoy the work of their hands.[37]

The charge against Woodsworth was subsequently dropped as the moneyed interests prevailed and crushed the strike. For our purposes, however, it is remarkable in context that this religious-political leader of what was seen to be a social revolution is placed under arrest for, among other things, citing this ancient poetic promise from Isa. 65:21-22.

That poem, in its scriptural context, of course had nothing to do with a Canadian labor conflict. It required no great interpretive ingenuity, however, to resituate those verses in the dispute between labor and moneyed interests, thus a usage not unlike that of Marx mentioned above. The verses of Isa. 65:21-22 concern property and assert that the possession and enjoyment of property shall be safe against any usurping seizure. The rereading by Woodsworth was telling. It was made more so by the reaction of the antistrike forces who in their context saw the biblical promise as a threat, because it witnessed against their rapacious economic activity. The phrasing is a libelous assertion, in the ears of those who valued an inequitable status quo and intended to protect it at all costs. A week after the arrest of Woodsworth, on June 25, the strikers returned to work. For the moment, the Isaiah text was defeated.

V

Isaiah 43:15-21 has become in important ways a pivotal text for the book of Isaiah, and indeed for the entire Old Testament/Hebrew Bible. Gerhard von Rad has made it the hinge whereby he programmatically linked the faith of Israel's Torah and the prophetic literature.[38] Brevard Childs has proposed that the accent on "new things" provides a large clue to the canonical structure of the book of Isaiah, so that "old things" refers to Isa. 1–39 and "new things" to Isa. 40–66.[39]

Our interest in this particular text, however, is of another order. The assertion of liberation rooted in God's resolve for the historical process, the governing theme of Isa. 40–55, makes this literature peculiarly important for African Americans who must deal theologically with the pervasive Western problem of white tyranny and specifically with the aggrieved reality of slavery in the United States. Brian K. Blount has reviewed in helpful detail the use of Scripture in black preaching and the way in which texts have been found to serve this distinctive and urgent agenda.[40]

It would be easiest to cite the remarkable work of Martin Luther King Jr. who made rich and imaginative use of Scripture in his cadences of liberation.[41] The problem in citing King, of course, is that to cite his work may be to engage in a kind of "exceptionalism" about King as a most peculiar and unparalleled voice in the African American community.

In fact, however, King's appropriation of Scripture with reference to African American freedom is not at all exceptional, but is rather characteristic. And therefore I cite a sermon by Beverly J. Shamana, "Letting Go," preaching on Isa. 43:15-21, though in fact she focuses upon vv. 18-19:

> Remember not the former things, nor consider the things of old.
> Behold, I am doing a new thing; now it springs forth, do you not perceive it?[42]

In referring to "former things," Shamana does not follow Childs in understanding this as Isa. 1–39 (judgment), but follows the more conventional understanding that "former things" are the Exodus events, a point, against Childs, seeming clear in this text.[43] More specifically, Shamana understands the "former things" to be "let go" as the "old baggage of slavery," or more precisely "a slave mentality."[44] The sermon is broadly based, so that it might address and appeal to many different listeners. Thus in her inventory of old things, she lists

- parents who failed to keep promises,
- a college education which promised a job,
- children who fail to be grateful,
- an attack of cancer, even though one is promised good health,
- a failed marriage.[45]

All of this is promised and has not been delivered, and so there is developed a sense of debit, of "being owed," and an accumulation of resentment. The preacher urges that "old things are to be forgotten."

For all of this generalization, however, there runs through the sermon the primary motif of the slave mentality of ancient Israel, and the parallel slave mentality of present-day African Americans who either are free and do not accept that freedom, or refuse the summons and effort to move toward freedom not yet in hand.

Midway through the sermon, Shamana speaks of being chained to the past, and then breaks out in,

"O freedom, O freedom, O freedom over me."

She asserts, "The indomitable human and divine alliance authored by God will not stay captive, will not be fettered." And then she moves to the fuller lyric:

> And before I'd be a slave
> I'd be buried in my grave;
> And go home to my Lord and be free.[46]

The sermon is concluded with the same phrasing.

Admittedly, the sermon treats freedom in a large and complex way. At the same time, however, we cannot doubt that the central issue and main current of the text is freedom for African Americans in a residue of slavery, which still continues its economic, political, and emotional power to define. Shamana has taken this text from Isaiah's (and Israel's) narrative of Jerusalem and has resituated it in the African American narrative of slavery and freedom. To be sure, the two narratives are intimately paralleled, so that this is not a surprising connection to make. Yet the two larger narratives are not the same. The current tension between Jews and African Americans in the United States may signal an important difference between the narratives, or at least a tension about who shall provide the governing interpretation, that is, "Who owns the text?"[47] Shamana, in any case, shows a compelling capacity to move the text from one narrative to another narrative without distortion, so that the ancient poem is concretely available for a new reading and for its fresh defining power in a quite different circumstance.

VI

The several usages of Isaiah I have cited evidence the ways in which Isaiah texts have been utilized in a wide variety of contexts. It is clear that these "text users" have permitted their own situations to determine the locus and intention of the text.[48] In each case, the text has been reread by being taken from the narrative of Israel's faith and its locus in the book of Isaiah, and recontextualized in a new interpretive situation of conflict.

Beyond a shared readiness to cite Isaiah, I can identify only one constant in these varied uses. In one form or another, all of these uses are in the service of protest on the side of transformation, against a status quo that resists truth "from below." Thus, Luther against the church's "theology of glory"; Marx against the political economy of the Rhineland

Diet, feminist readers against a patriarchal reductionism which produces despair, or with Mary Gordon, against an abusive reality of distorted motherhood; Woodsworth against an exploitative labor system; and Shamana against the residue of slavery.

Perhaps all of these rereaders have rightly sensed something about the radical quality of the book of Isaiah, rooted in the holiness of God and addressed to "live in human society."

To be sure, my approach is somewhat subjective, depending upon the happenstance of specific cases I am able to cite. My hope is to suggest in a convincing way that along with our ongoing critical work and the emerging claim of "canon criticism," we must pay attention to a third enterprise: practical usage, which reflects upon the intuitive ways in which texts are understood to perform "in human society." I suggest that a study of these usages is not in conflict with more intentional critical study, but is complementary. This third enterprise, reflecting the continuing authority of the Bible as "social code," from time to time suggests hermeneutical access points to which scholarly attention must be paid.[49] The uses I have cited reflect not only a "high view" of Scripture, but also a continued valuing of the cadences and rhetoric of the text. Such usage asserts the ongoing pertinence for "human society" of the One to whom these texts bear witness and through which that One becomes present.

3
The Prophetic Word of God and History

THE CLAIM THAT "GOD ACTS IN HISTORY" IS NOT COMPATIBLE WITH OUR Enlightenment notions of control, reason, objectivity, and technique.[1] Indeed, if one begins with the assumptions of modernity, history can only be a bare story of power, in which the God of the Bible can never make a significant appearance. The claim that "God acts in history" requires a very different beginning point. In the end, the claim that God's word impinges upon human history is a counterclaim refusing the common debate concerning whether history is a tale of either raw power or blind faith.[2] The claim that God's word impinges upon the human process rejects both options of raw power and silly supernaturalism.

1

A prophetic understanding of the historical process must make its way against two competitors. First, there are the temptations of modernity, which have perhaps been embodied in the "doctrine" of Henry Kissinger.[3] This view assumes that the historical process is essentially a closed process in which one must manage the available pieces as best as one can, because there will be no new pieces. This view has emptied the historical process of inscrutability and mystery, and it seeks to eradicate ambiguity. It has concluded that "might makes right," that "history is written by the winners," and that history is simply "the story of the state," that is, the story of power concentrated in the hands of those who deserve it, who can manage it well, and who benefit from it. This view of history is powerful among us, reflecting our fear of and our sense of our cosmic homelessness; this view drives the arms race and ends in despair that brutalizes, either in the name of the state or against the claims of the state.

Second, and in an odd alliance with the first view, is an older religious view of the historical process that affirms that all of life is in the hands of the gods (or God), that humankind may propose but God disposes, and that therefore human choice in the end does not matter. This kind of supernaturalism that eventuates in fatalism and is manifested in astrology leads to an abdication of human responsibility and human freedom. It invites despair on the one hand and recklessness on the other, because God will finally decide.

I submit that it is the first of these views that is most powerful among us, and that the latter has little attraction for us if it is spelled out with any precision. In fact, however, these two views converge in a massive verdict of despair. Whereas the former believes that human power is all, the latter acknowledges that in the end human power and human effort are futile. Together these two options lead to a historical process that is essentially fated, in which there are no important possibilities that lie beyond our several necessities. One may be fated to terrible power or one may be fated to miserable helplessness, but in either case fated. I submit that for those struggling for faith in our society, these are the two large, most visible, and available options.

II

Our theme, "prophetic word of God and history," begins at a different place, in a different mode of discourse, though with a very different epistemology.[4] This theme refuses the modernist reduction of history to power; it equally refuses the religious temptation of supernaturalism. It begins with stunned, unjustified, unargued speech of affirmation and celebration that asserts and testifies to the intrusion, surprise, discontinuity, gifts, judgment, newness, and ambiguity that are present in the midst of the human process. That is, it insists on speaking precisely about those matters that the other two views of the human process want to deny. That stunned, unjustified, unargued speech is human speech, filled with daring hutzpah and focused with scandalous particularity. This speech is so daring as to specify concrete places where the presence, purpose, and reality of God's "otherness" make decisive inroads on the human process, either in friendly or in hostile ways. That is, it names the places where intrusion, gift, ambiguity, and newness are present, and it gives to those happenings the name of holiness, either holy graciousness or holy judgment.

There is, in my judgment, no way to understand prophetic speech (or prophetic ministry) without going back to the very old, very deep, very odd Jewish rootage of such speech. Indeed, "prophetic" is a mode of dangerous Jewishness in a safety-seeking world of imperial certitude. This Jewish claim is that history does not begin in power plays or in "natural" origins, but in miracles that are discerned, construed, celebrated, and confessed in stunned faith.

1. The test case I cite is the conversation of Abraham, Sarah, and the three messengers in Gen. 18:1-15.[5] The visitors announce that Sarah will have a baby in her old age. Sarah snickers in disbelief. In a cutting rebuke to Sarah, the visitor responds, "Is anything too difficult for God?" The word "difficult" (or too hard, too wondrous, too impossible) is the Hebrew word *pela'*. The means whereby Abraham and Sarah receive an inexplicable future is through a *pela'*, through an emergent occurrence that they and their world had defined as impossible. History, that is, the liberated transactions of human freedom and human possibility, does not begin through

human initiatives or acts of courage or cleverness, but in an inexplicable turn that prophetic faith confesses to be the work of God, a work that stands outside the expectation, prediction, and horizon of human control. Indeed, one can argue that human history persists because this God who visited Abraham and Sarah and who worked a *pela'* continues to keep open historical, human possibilities beyond all human expectation. While our fearful human propensity is to close down the historical prospect, it is the work of this God and the speech of this God that keep the historical horizon open.

2. This narrative speech of Gen. 18:1-15 concerning miracle secures its focus for ancient Israel in the exodus narrative of Exod. 1–15, which is the world's primal *pela'*. In that event (regularly reenacted in Passover liturgy), the tight birth control of the Egyptian empire is broken (compare Exod. 1:15-22), and a new people is formed in the world of empires, a people with no clear historical antecedents.[6] Out of the promissory word of God, this people appears as a *novum*, a new phenomenon, in the history of the world. This people is set free for covenantal relations, for obedience to the Torah, a charter for human equity, justice, and dignity. Martin Buber has said of the inexplicable event of the Exodus that it is a miracle marked by "abiding astonishment."[7] That is, the exodus is a known happening that continues to give off power and to claim attention and allegiance. It has a power that continues to stun and to keep the world open. It refuses the closed definitions of what is possible, definitions that are coercively imposed by the empires of the world. Michael Walzer, moreover, has shown that this *pela'* of the exodus has continued to be a remarkable engine for revolutionary newness in the world, continuing to enliven and authorize subversive futures against every status quo.[8]

Notice that this originating event, the generation of a new community in the world, is opposed to modernity's reduction of history to power, for Pharaoh had all the power and could not prevail. Notice that this originating event is also opposed to an easy supernaturalism, for it is essentially a human act whereby Moses (and Aaron) confront Pharaoh and lead a "long march" to freedom.[9] That is, the decisive show of God's power is mediated through the actions and speech of Moses. It is the convergence of holy resolve and human courage that initiates a newness that the empire cannot understand and cannot resist.

3. Out of the narrative of newness to Abraham and Sarah, and out of the Mosaic event of liberation, comes Israel's prophetic tradition. In this community, there is a series of speakers, human speakers, emboldened by holiness, who dared envision scenarios of possibility that "the rulers of this age" had declared to be impossible. On the one hand, these prophets dared to envision a terrible impossibility, that God's own people would answer for their cynical, willful disobedience and come to a suffering end. On the other hand, these prophets dared to imagine a totally new beginning, whereby

God would re-form his people in exile, to create, as there had not been, a people after God's own heart. They dared to speak of "plucking up and tearing down, of planting and building" (Jer. 1:10). They dared to speak what their contemporaries thought either craziness (compare Hosea 9:7) or treason (compare Jer. 38:4). They dared to voice what power had nullified and what fate had settled. And in their speaking, they worked a newness.

4. It is through this tradition of new possibilities that the early church understood Jesus. They saw in him wonders worked and impossibilities enacted. Power for newness swirled about him that establishment authority could neither resist nor nullify. Through his presence the lame walked, the deaf heard, the lepers were cleansed, the dead were raised, and the poor had their debts canceled (Luke 7:22-23). In the end, the church was persuaded and confessed that even death could not hold him (Acts 2:24).

It is clear that the beginning point of this theme for Christians is the claim that Jesus is a full embodiment of the prophetic tradition of the Old Testament. Jesus speaks and enacts the holy word of God in ways that "pluck up and tear down," that "plant and build." It is equally clear that the church's discernment and articulation of Jesus do not stop with this characteristically Jewish understanding. The church has gone further to confess that Jesus is not only an *utterer* of the word, but is himself the *uttered* word. That is, Jesus' own person is God's word of life, which shatters all idolatrous forms of life and makes new community possible.

The church accomplished this articulation, which is radically Jewish and which moves beyond Jewish prophetic categories, through the formula "word becomes flesh," or in its more metaphysical assertion, "two natures in one person." Even such a formulation as this latter one, however, does not depart from our primary acknowledgment that prophetic speech is *human utterance* of *holy word*. Christians affirm therefore that Jesus' life is indeed a human utterance, an utterance of the very word, will, purpose, and intent of God. The recurring temptation of the Christian tradition is to remove this word from the public process, either into private spirituality or into theological ontology away from public issues. Such temptations misread both Jesus as the church experienced him, and the Jewish tradition, which is decisive for understanding him. It is the claim of prophetic Christology (as it is of Jewish prophetic faith) that God's abiding intention for creation becomes operative precisely in the midst of suffering, and visible primarily in the hope-filled emergence of public newness.

I do not argue that Jewish prophecy must come to a christological conclusion. Rather, I assert simply that Jesus of Nazareth cannot be understood except in the rhetoric and epistemology of Jewish prophecy, which refuses escapist reductionisms, either into privatism or ontology, and which attends to scandalous newness wrought by the power of God.

III

The courage and burden of these speakers of scandalous impossibility is to find speech that is adequate for the character of God. There are no prophets (as here understood) without this God who is the subject of their speech, and there is no prophetic word except that this is a God of whom it is said, "thus saith the LORD." That is, human utterance sounds holy speech. Thus, for all our interest in sociology and politics, our theme is a theological one about the character of God and the courage to bring this God to speech.[10] What the prophets assert is that human processes and policies, apart from this God, are wrongly construed. I suggest three ways of speaking about this God who keeps the human process open to possibility. The character of this God who does wonders (pela'th) is enunciated one oracle at a time, one crisis at a time, one possibility at a time:

• This God, unlike other gods, is *holy*, brooking no rivals, utterly unapproachable. There is at the center of the historical process a force and a will that cannot be harnessed, domesticated, manipulated, or bought off.

• This God, unlike other gods, is a *"lover of justice"* (Ps. 99:4), intolerant of injustice, mightily at work in the public processes of history, allied with the powerless, critical of the greedy powerful, intervening with a "preferential option for the poor."

• This God, unlike other gods, because holy and because just, is a *dangerous, subversive God,* unsettling every status quo that offends holiness and that mocks justice. This God, unlike any other, is one who subverts, ending what is cherished, beginning what we little expect, in order that the world may receive and enact its proper life as God's creation.

The prophetic word in history is human utterance about this God unintimidated by modernity, unimpressed by excessive religion, nonnegotiable about rhetoric, nondefensive about its epistemology, daring to insist that this God who works wonders in the historical process is still at large, liberating and healing.

IV

Speech about this God, speech that is daringly human and embarrassingly particular, regularly sounds themes that demand attention and require a re-visioning of the human process. I will identify five such themes that are characteristic of the prophets, though many others might be cited.

1. Out of God's unaccommodating holiness, the prophetic word is *against idols,* and consequently against self-serving, self-deceiving ideology.[11] Idolatry and its twin, ideology, always want to absolutize some arrangement of power and knowledge, so that we may bow down to the work of our hands. Against such an absolutizing pretension, the holiness of God critiques, exposes, and assaults every phony absolute, for all such supposed absolutes of nation, race, party, or sex will end in death.

2. This holy God *refuses then to absolutize the present,* any present. This holy God drives always toward a new unsettling, unsettled future, which is not yet visible, when God's purpose will be worked and God's regime fully established. That threatening, promising future that lives on the lips of prophets warns against taking the present with excessive seriousness, even if it is a present that we happen to value inordinately.

3. Out of God's justice, prophetic speech characteristically speaks about *human suffering.* It takes human suffering as a definitional datum of the human, historical process. Thus, already in the exodus narrative, when Israel cries out, God sees, God hears, God knows, God remembers, God intervenes (Exod. 2:23-25; 3:7-14).[12] It is the utterance of hurt that moves God to newness. The powers of modernity do not want to notice human suffering, but to define suffering as a legitimate and necessary cost of well-being or as an inexplicable given of human history. Prophetic speech demystifies pain and sees clearly that much pain is principally caused by the manipulation of economic and political access whereby the strong regularly destroy the weak. Such suffering is not a legitimate, bearable cost, and it is not inexplicable. Social pain rather is a product of social relationships, which can be transformed. Prophetic speech focused in hurt speaks against any tidy administration of social relations that crushes human reality in the interest of order, progress, profit, or "the common good."

4. Out of God's justice, prophetic speech characteristically takes *a critical posture over against established power.* Established power in predictable ways always manages to legitimate itself, until it drives every other factor out of the social equation, and history comes to equal not only the play of power, but finally the embrace of this particular arrangement of power.

Prophetic speech refuses such a seductive domestication of the historical process. Prophetic speech not only insists that the raw use of power is wrong and must pay heed to human reality, it also makes the more difficult claim that, in the end, raw power cannot succeed and is not the final datum of human history. Prophetic speech is realistic in knowing that massive power matters enormously; it is equally insistent that massive power does not matter ultimately, concerning the outcome or significance of the human process. This assertion about power is not an obscurantist supernaturalism that bails out with reference to God. Rather it is the studied conclusion that there simply is not enough power in the long run to sustain itself in the face of human restlessness among those who refuse to be eradicated as an inconvenience. This human restlessness that refuses eradication, moreover, is rooted in God's own resolve for the world.

5. Prophetic speech, finally, is not an act of criticism. It is rather *an act of relentless hope that refuses despair,* that refuses to believe that the world is closed off in patterns of exploitation and oppression.[13] It refuses a closed present tense that is excessively complacent with the current social rela-

tions, or excessively despairing about an unbearable present tense. This speech knows that such closed-off life inevitably produces brutality, the child of despair, either out of strident control or out of hopelessness. It dares to assert in any and every circumstance the conviction known since Abraham and Sarah and since Moses and Aaron, namely, that there is a God who can and will make all things new, even in the face of our most closed-down, self-satisfied present tense. This is what the text means when it asserts that God works an impossibility in order that "all the earth may know that there is a God in Israel" (1 Sam. 17:46).

V

It is obvious that our theme is not contained in ancient questions of prophetic rhetoric. The theme in its powerful contemporaneity is focused, rather, on a very present-tense struggle among us. The issue I suggest is this: Could this prophetic faith rooted in old treasured texts be credible in our situation? Could it be credible against dominant theories of raw power and against current practices of pious abdication? The question is a difficult one, and I want to provide no easy answer. I can, however, suggest four elements in an affirmative answer that may permit our embrace of the prophetic tradition as viable and credible.

1. The issue is first of all not, "Is God's word powerful in the historical process?" That is to engage in a metaphysical speculation for which there can be no clear answer. Rather, I suggest a very proximate question, which in some ways is easier and in some ways is more demanding. I pose the question this way: "Can the synagogue and the church, the communities committed to this prophetic claim, do the hard, demanding intellectual, rhetorical work that will construe the world according to this memory and this discourse?" That is, the question is not a question about God, but about our courage and imagination. It is not a question of speculation, but of practice. Can these communities of faith (and their ordained leaders) find tongues and ears and will to embrace, articulate, and enact an odd, particular, scandalous mode of reality against the powerful reductionisms all around us?

Thus I submit that the crisis of "word and history" is not that God has become obsolete or discredited with the rise of modernity, but that these communities of odd discourse, entrusted with such speech, have compromised their vision and domesticated their passion. Where such speaking stops, the word ends its intrusive say in human history. The pastoral task, then, is the recovery of such discourse in quite concrete ways. Note well that the issue is not heroic courage by pastor or rabbi, but an entire community of circumcised/baptized believers who trust its own way of speech. The issue of such peculiarity is not unlike the maintenance of Jewish discourse in a world of Hellenism; there is now a struggle for discourse that besets both Jews and Christians in an intellectually leveling, particularity-denying culture.[14]

2. The odd moment in which the world finds itself does not amount to "proof" that the word of God governs history. "Proof" is neither sought nor offered on such an issue and is indeed a misleading category. Indeed that category is a product of modernity. Nonetheless, recent events in Eastern Europe and South Africa make unmistakably clear that there are public possibilities that emerge and erupt well beyond any option entertained by established power. Moreover, it is astonishing that the word—on the lips of poets and novelists and visionaries—has characteristically played such a crucial role in these turns of human affairs. We have witnessed the odd reality that the word has turned out to be more compelling and powerful than tanks or guns or secret police. Wherever that happens, it is a miracle, that is, a happening that contains "abiding astonishment."[15] We do not understand how such a happening can occur; we only notice that it does happen. It becomes unmistakably evident that such brutalizing, despairing, concentrations of power in terms of secret police, tanks, and guns do not possess the means of coercion or intimidation to stay the holy power of justice that subverts all dehumanizing status quo.

It takes no great imagination, in these specific cases, to see that daring speech can and does cause the fall and rise of public order. Indeed, in the cases of Eastern Europe and South Africa, it takes enormous resolve to read such events apart from an affirmation of the word impinging upon history. Thus I suggest that the events of our recent past do indeed constitute evidence that all our powerful technique has not banished and cannot banish the powerful, holy word uttered by human lips in the matrix of suffering and hope. Israel is the one who first enacted such odd power where there is the convergence of holy resolve and human utterance.

3. But of course most of us are not placed by God to live and believe in Eastern Europe or in South Africa. Ours is a more difficult place, and we are always tempted to imagine that were we somewhere else, things would be more obvious and compelling. It may be that the ethos and lack of serious discourse in the culture matrix of the United States makes ours a most difficult environment in which to utter such holy words. For all our talk about "freedom of speech," it is the case that serious human discourse has all but disappeared among us. Issues are not much joined among us. Serious hope is scarcely practiced. Deep hurt is largely unacknowledged. Ours is a most co-opted climate for humanness, besotted as we are with power, arrogant in our greed, confident in our technology, still belatedly determined to work our powerful will in the world, characteristically on the side of brutalizing power. It would be ironic indeed if in this society so impressed with "freedom of speech" that in fact holy speech of abiding astonishment could be completely obliterated among us by technique.[16] The cost of such

"progress" is enormous, even if little noticed. The cost comes in the disappearance of a human infrastructure, in the erosion of public institutions of justice, health, and education, in the emergence of a permanent and growing underclass; the ultimate cost is an absence of political will to match resource to need. Indeed, the drastic separation of resource from need in our society is done almost with the arrogance of virtue, the virtue of a nullified compassion. The outcome of such a procedure is the breakdown of persons, families, communities, and institutions, the near disappearance of what is humanness.

If one asks how that destructive process can be countered or subverted in our society, it seems clear that it will not happen, in the first instance, by great programs or strategies, but by utterance unafraid, speech that brings holiness back into history, that lets justice sound in the presence of power, that owns suffering even in a climate of apathy, that voices hope in the midst of despair, that finally refuses brutality in the name of the coming rule of God. Thus for us, called to faith and life here, our theme is not an interesting intellectual question, but an issue of our vocation and our common future. The prophetic tradition, however, has always surfaced with speech in the most difficult contexts—and this is our "most difficult context."

4. The issue of a history-making word is not an intellectual question about whether modern people can believe ancient claims. It is a political question of what kind of power has power for life.[17] It is a question of rhetoric; can concrete speech, which utters the sounds of human passion, have a hearing in the midst of technological speech? Most of all, it is an intellectual question about the premises of human life that are to prevail among us.

The technological effort to silence and overcome awkward human-holy speech is not a neutral, value-free, modest proposal.[18] It is a deeply partisan enterprise. What passes for objectivity is in fact a massive ideological claim that need not to be respected as objective, but critiqued as a false ideological proposal for reality.[19]

I suspect that prophetic speech, that is, history-making, human-holy speech about hurt and hope, has disappeared because we have accepted the pretensions of technological silence.[20] Our proper task, in the tradition of Israel's prophets, is not excessive respect for the silence of technique, but exposure of that silence for what it is, a surreptitious, determined resolve to end the rhetorical-political process that makes human life possible, that lets God be present and effective among us. Practitioners of this Jewish, prophetic tradition are in a polemical situation that requires naming the destructive option now so powerful and providing a serious, positive alternative.[21]

Clearly, the main body of church and synagogue little suspects the emergency situation of faith in which we find ourselves. The outcome of the struggle between *prophetic utterance,* which enlivens, and *technological silence,* which censures, depends upon those who care to join an issue in order to help the faithful see that our God-given humanness will not last long beyond or outside this dangerous tradition of speech. Where such rhetoric is stilled, our humanness is increasingly nullified. The intellectual challenge is not to provide a rhetorical addendum to our technological orientation, but to counter it from the ground up.

VI

Conclusion: In the face of the collapse of Soviet Communism, Francis Fukuyama has proclaimed the "end of history."[22] By this he suggests that democratic capitalism has established a permanent ideological hegemony in the world. Such an assertion is, on the face of it, false, dangerous, even absurd. It is an ideological claim farcically masquerading as nonideology, in order to banish the reality of "class" from political consideration. Such an "end of history" happens only when holy-human speech is lost. I submit that the prophetic word of God is the unending, resilient minority insistence that power cannot finally drive out human hurt and human hope. Note well, I do not suggest that "prophetic speech" is some grand supernaturalism that invites theological obscurantism. Nor does prophetic speech consist in making predictions; nor is prophetic speech "social action."

Prophetic speech, that is, the way God's word impinges upon human history, is concrete talk in particular circumstances where the large purposes of God for the human enterprise come down to particulars of hurt and healing, of despair and hope. The synagogue and church have this demanding, awkward task of claiming much more than can be explained. What we have to say is rooted in textual memory and is driven by present pain. This speech insists that the processes of public power where such speech is nullified are a false reality that cannot endure. We bear witness that what we know and utter is not only dangerous and subversive, but also life-giving. About the riddle of power, truth, and holiness, we echo the odd conclusion of the book of Proverbs, so evident in the world where history has not ended:

> No wisdom, no understanding, no counsel
> can avail against the LORD.
> The horse is made ready for the day of battle,
> but the victory belongs to the LORD. (Prov. 21:30-31)[23]

4

The "Baruch Connection": Reflections on Jeremiah 43:1-7

WE ARE ONLY AT THE BEGINNING OF OUR ATTEMPT TO UNDERSTAND THE canonical shape of the book of Jeremiah. It is clear that the three-source hypothesis of Mowinckel and Duhm continues to hold scholarship in thrall. Not only has "source analysis" dominated recent discussion, but scholars have most often insisted upon asking not only questions about literary sources, but also questions about the historicity of those who purport to author the sources. Thus the recent comprehensive and impressive commentaries of Holladay and Carroll not only articulate the extreme limits of such source analysis, but they are in fact twinned in their preoccupation with historical questions.[1] Whereas Holladay voices a maximalist claim for the historical Jeremiah, Carroll is concerned to deny any claim for the availability of historical Jeremiah in the text, in the interest of his larger concern to establish the Deuteronomic shape of the book.[2] While Carroll comes closer to issues of canonical shape than does Holladay, this is largely inadvertent. Carroll has no interest that I can discern in the canonical shape; the reason he comes closer than Holladay is only because of his interest in moving as far away as possible from historical Jeremiah. Thus he draws more and more of the text later, closer in time to the final shapers of the book. To be sure, Carroll and Holladay cannot be faulted for not addressing canonical questions, since that is neither their interest nor intention. I begin here only in order to observe that recent scholarship, dominated as it is by these two commentaries, is of little help for the matter before us.[3]

1

Concerning the question of canonical shape, I mention four pertinent matters. First, A. R. Diamond, Kathleen O'Connor, and Mark Smith have begun an investigation of the role of the so-called "lamentations of Jeremiah" in the canonical form of the text.[4] Unfortunately, they have confined themselves to that part of the book of Jeremiah in which those poems occur, and do not venture into the more comprehensive issues of the canonical shape of the book. Second, I suspect that McKane's notion of "rolling corpus" is pertinent to our question;[5] it is, however, not very well developed, and thus far McKane has pursued canonical issues in any intentional way. Third, Childs has provided a rich but inchoate suggestion about "two forms of proclamation" concerning early/late, oral/written, poetry/prose, judgment/promise[6] (on which see the paradigm proposed by Ronald E. Clements[7]). But Childs has done little specific textual work to show how the broad claims of a canonical structure work out in detail. Fourth, Christopher R. Seitz has considered the ways in which the book deliberately juxtaposes tensions with opposing interpretive views.[8] In my judgment, however, Seitz has only identified the materials out of which a canonical reflection must be pursued. Thus, while there are important hints and beginnings in present scholarship, the question of canonical process and shape still awaits a more sustained address.

II

The purpose of this chapter is to suggest that the person of "Baruch," and particularly Baruch in 43:1-7, may be understood as a key to the canonizing process and shape of the material. That is, the interest that seems to be represented by Baruch in the text seems congruent with that redactional community that shaped the final form of the text. This congruence makes it possible to see something of canonical intentionality in the character of Baruch.[9] (Here I shall be concerned with the shape of the Masoretic Text [MT].)[10] Of course, reference to Baruch is not a new suggestion; I intend, however, to consider Baruch not as an editor, author, or redactor, but as a character in the text, whose role may suggest something of the intention of the shapers of the book.

Focus on Baruch is in and of itself problematic. At the outset, by "Baruch" I do not refer to the so-called "Baruch source,"[11] but to the explicit references to him in the text. On the one hand, Baruch is not mentioned often in the book. Of the four references, 43:1-7, my text of focus, is least addressed in scholarly discussion. The other three references include the two narratives about the purchase of Jeremiah's land inheritance (chapter 32) and the burning of the scroll (chapter 36), and the oracle concerning the destiny of Baruch (chapter 45). Thus attention to 43:1-7 may be a focus on what appears to be a minor text, even for the character of Baruch.

On the other hand, scholars have not been able to resolve the issue of the historicity of the person of Baruch. Holladay follows a long-established consensus in taking what seem to be historical allusions to Baruch at face value.[12] In that reading, Baruch and his brother Seraiah (compare 51:59) may be understood as "members of a family prominent at the royal court." That consensus about the historicity of Baruch has been sharply challenged by Carroll, who finds in Baruch a fictional character whereby the "tradition created and developed a subsidiary figure to accompany Jeremiah."[13] Carroll seems to vacillate between a verdict that Baruch was "created" out of whole cloth, and a contention that he is a secondary, minor "aleatory" figure who has been made large by the tradition. Carroll's point, I take it, is that Baruch is to be seen not simply as a historical agent, as though our text is simply reportage, but as a carrier of the ideological interests of the Deutero-nomic tradition. When seen in that context, I suspect it does not matter much to Carroll whether Baruch was or was not a historical person, as long as primary accent is given to him as an ideological carrier and cipher.

The most important and serious response to Carroll's dismissal of "his-torical" Baruch is that of J. Andrew Dearman, who asserts that "there is no good reason historically or culturally to doubt the existence or the actuality of Baruch and certain other scribal officials named as sympathetic to Jere-miah."[14] I am inclined to think that Dearman's case for "historicity" is a compelling one. That, however, does not diminish Carroll's main point that Baruch is cast in the text in the service of "scribal-Deuteronomic ideology." Indeed, Dearman seems to concede as much at the end of his notes, where he speaks of "evidence for the circle of scriptural editors/authors common-ly known as the Deuteronomistic historians."[15]

In the end, in my judgment, the issue of historicity is completely unim-portant for our purposes. It matters not at all whether Baruch is a fictive vehicle for an ideology or a historical personality in the background of the present book of Jeremiah. In either case, his presence as a character with-in the text is in the service of a specific ideology, which may stand in ten-sion with historical Jeremiah but which pervades the canonical book of Jeremiah. I do not think, however, that simply identifying "ideology" as a force in the present book of Jeremiah is the end of the matter. Rather, we must scrutinize more carefully the meaning of the term "ideology," and the substance of this particular ideology, if "Baruch" is to help us read the book of Jeremiah in its final form and in its final intentionality.

III

The text of 43:1-7 reflects a dispute in the community about how to respond to the announced threat of Babylon.[16] As it is presented, the debate turns on whether to stay in Jerusalem (which means submitting to the invading power of Babylon) or to flee to Egypt. The dispute about adher-ence to one superpower or the other was a long-standing one, reflected, as Seitz has shown, in the varying influence of the several sons of Josiah and their respective mothers.[17] It is to be noted that in the book of Jeremiah, the dispute takes two sequential forms. In its earlier form, the issue is whether to *submit* willingly to Babylon or to *stand in resistance* in Jerusalem (38:17-18). The second, later form of the same dispute, reflected in our text, repre-sents a fall-back position after it had become clear that Jerusalem would be taken, that is, after resistance in Jerusalem had become futile. Now, with resistance no longer an option, the debate is whether *to stay* in submission or *to flee* to Egypt (42:9-17). In both phases of the dispute about policy, Jeremiah (the person or the book) takes the position more sympathetic to cooperation with Babylon, first *not to resist* in Jerusalem and then *not to flee* to Egypt but to remain in the city. The counteropinion, reflected by the opponents of the book of Jeremiah, is first *to resist* and then *to flee*. (It is important for our purposes that both of these assertions [38:17-18; 42:9-17] are already cast in prose.)

The two phases of this dispute are evidenced in two heavy-handed oracles placed in the mouth of Jeremiah. The first, concerning whether to submit or resist, is given in 38:17-18 with a double "if-then" phrasing. The positive outcome of surrender for Zedekiah is that "your life shall be spared, and this city shall not be burned with fire, and you and your houses shall live" (v. 17). The negative outcome of resistance is massive destruction with no escape (v. 18). The strategic question of policy is cast as a severe theological choice.

In the second policy decision (42:9-17), to which our text of 43:1-7 is a response, the issues are again given in an "if-then" formulation. The positive "if-then" formulation in vv. 10-12 concerns remaining in the city and receiving mercy (from Yahweh and from the king of Babylon) and restoration. The negative alternative is more complex, because it contains a subsidiary "if-then" formula in vv. 15b-17. But the negative outcome is the same, an intense rhetorical effort culminating in death by sword, famine, and pestilence (vv. 16-17).

Thus, in both parts of the policy dispute, cooperation with Babylon is given by the Jeremiah tradition as a chance for survival, but resistance to Babylon is given in divine oracle as a sure way to death.

IV

After the demanding options of 42:9-17 given as divine oracle, which is reinforced by the assertion of 42:18-22 reiterating the threat of sword, famine, and pestilence, we arrive at the confrontation of 43:1-7. The opponents to Jeremiah's recommended policy of submission and continuation in the city, the advocates of flight to Egypt (in this partisan rendering called "insolent" [zed]), respond. They declare that the prophetic counsel to remain in submission to Babylon is a lie, that is, a false policy. The word used here is the same as is the one earlier preferred by Jeremiah in 23:16-22, when he accuses his opponents of falseness.[18] There the false prophets are accused of speaking "visions of their own minds," stubbornly following "their own stubborn hearts" (23:16-17).

What is most striking in the parallel between the indictment of Jeremiah in our passage with the dismissive term *šqr* and Jeremiah's indictment in 23:16-22[19] is that Jeremiah is not accused of speaking "visions of his own mind" nor following his own "stubborn heart." Rather, the cause of the lie is Baruch! It is the vision of *his* mind and *his* stubborn heart that stands indicted.

As the book of Jeremiah has it, this rejection of Jeremiah's counsel (or the counsel of Baruch, as the opponents put it) and the defiant flight to Egypt (48:8-13; 44:1-23, 24-30)lead to a massive prophetic threat against Egypt and against those of Jerusalem who flee there. In 43:10-13, Nebuchadnezzar is specifically named as the "devastator" of Egypt.[20] In 44:30-31, the destroyer is unnamed, but the destruction in Egypt will happen "just as" Nebuchadnezzar devastated Jerusalem at the behest of Yahweh. In the imaginative construal of historical reality, as shaped by the canonizers of the book of Jeremiah, this devastating, deathly return to Egypt brings the story of Yahweh's life with Israel full circle from the exodus, so that this foolish choice is presented as the negation and nullification of the entire story of rescue that constituted Israel.[21] Thus a public crisis, seen in larger theological context, is read as a negative counterpoint to Israel's primal credo and self-understanding. (See the exodus rhetoric used negatively in 21:5.)

What interests us here, however, is that the opponents of the warning of Jeremiah given in 42:8-17 refuse the work of Jeremiah and credit that rejected counsel to Baruch instead. Two questions arise from this exchange, both of which directly concern canonical matters.

First, what does this charge tell us about the relation between Jeremiah and "Baruch?" (Note that I allow for the role of Baruch to be fictive, following Carroll.) We may take Jeremiah to be a prophetic figure who anguishes over the ruin of Jerusalem, and who discerns in it the hidden but decisive resolve of Yahweh. It is exactly poetic idiom that permits the interpretation of public event in terms of divine resolve. (Indeed, it is clear that as soon as the elusiveness of poetry is reduced to prose, the theological judgments made are open to a very different kind of political dispute.) The speech most characteristically assigned to the poet Jeremiah (perhaps also fictively constructed) is intensely Yahwistic, imaginatively poetic, and almost completely lacking in specific sociopolitical references. This is not to say that "Jeremiah" was not aware of political matters or disinterested. But his poetry avoids specifically political commentary or even recommendation. That is, it is plausible that Jeremiah, with a poetic-Yahwistic discernment, was largely "innocent" of concrete sociopolitical intent and unencumbered by policy *Tendenz,* so intense was he about the Yahwistic theological crisis, letting the political implications of his words fall out as they would. (I do not suggest that anyone, least of all such a daring poet, is ever completely innocent; relatively speaking, however, the poetry is surely restrained about lending itself to any blatant concrete propagandistic effort. It is important to notice precisely how I mean "innocent." The difference between the poetry and prose in this matter is not a subjective or interpretive judgment. It is the case that the poetry lacks political specificity.) While such a poet could not be unaware of the political interests served by the poetry, it is credible to think that the interests thus served neither evoked nor legitimated the prophetic utterance, so fixed was he upon the covenantal tradition and the claims of Yahweh in that tradition.[22]

In contrast to Jeremiah, who in 43:1-7 is not the target of attack, the accusation leveled against Baruch is that Baruch is not an "innocent," disinterested Yahwist, but is party to the sociopolitical dispute, and an adversary of those here called "insolent." That is, we may imagine that Baruch is deeply involved in quarrels about policy that are never disinterested. If this is a correct identification of the (fictive?) character of Baruch, then we have a relation between a poet whose words address metapolitical issues and a much interested political "user" of his Yahwistic poetry.

The relation between the two characters (which has spin-off value with regard to their conventionally designated literary sources, respectively A and B-C) thus is an asymmetrical one. I therefore suggest more or less politically *"innocent" and unencumbered poetry* of anguish and discernment is taken up and utilized for a *political opinion*. That is, the poetry taken up is understood by its political user not as a distortion, but as an "application," concrete explication of what is implicit in the poetry. Given the poetry, so the "users" may have concluded, it can have no other political import than the one they give it. There is inevitably, to be sure, a very different texture to the unencumbered poetry and the practical usage of it. For the practical usage of such anguished articulation and anticipation is never innocent, unambiguous, or disinterested. It is in the nature of the interpretive maneuver toward specificity that it cannot be otherwise. The opponents of this peculiar, asymmetrical relation between poet and political operative (Baruch) reverse the process and suggest that the poet is not only "used" by, but is motivated and counseled by, the political operative. This polemic against the poet along with the political advocate is a common strategy of "the opposition," who characteristically misunderstand that such poetry can be innocent and unencumbered, and yet "useful" for more concrete purposes.

Second, one may wonder why the "insolent men" take up this form of accusation. Why did they not directly accuse Jeremiah more insistently? It may be that the poet himself is too much beyond reproach for such a charge to be credible, for perhaps he is vindicated by events. Perhaps Jeremiah was so protected as pro-Babylonian that he is unassailable. Or it may be that Jeremiah's own "non-applied" utterances simply do not justify such a charge. Or it may be that Baruch, and all that he represents, is simply an easier target, and that it is the political operators and not the poet whom they want to get. Such a scenario presses us a second time to the question, who is Baruch? I intend to bracket out historical issues about his person and ask what interests he serves and embodies in the text. Here I believe that Dearman helps us greatly. He proposes that the families of Shaphan, who several times is the great public defender of Jeremiah and his disputed message, and Neraiah, whose sons Baruch and Seraiah figure in the scrolls of Jeremiah, are in fact influential scribal families.

Once we are past the historical questions, the arguments of Dearman and Carroll, in my judgment, tend to converge and agree. On the one hand, these families *exercise enormous public influence*. (Here again I allow the textual sketch to be fictive, though no doubt reflective of actual public forces.) On the other hand, they *respond affirmatively to the poetic-Yahwistic discernment of reality offered by Jeremiah*. These families, or the scribal-Deuteronomic forces they embody and represent, occupy a middle position between Jeremiah's poetry (which is not designed to be politically "useful") and realpolitik (which is not seriously occupied with the religious claims of Yahwism).

V

I suggest that these families, or those interests they represent and embody, occupy a delicate middle ground, which refuses both "innocent religion" and cynical politics. They affirm that Jeremiah's "innocent" rhetoric speaks a truth that effectively impinges upon the political reality. They accept the poetry as germane to public policy and practice, I imagine, not simply because they are pious, but, as is always the case when religion sounds politically credible, because the poetry at least in part coheres with vested interest and perceived interest.[23]

I do not suggest that this is an act of preemptive "bad faith," but an act of good faith "realism." It is for this reason that Jeremiah's words, when "applied" in more concrete ways by the Baruch party, are contentious, given other political interests with other judgments about what is faithful and pragmatic. Thus, as understood by scribal-Deuteronomic opinion, I do not conclude that staying in Jerusalem rather than fleeing to Egypt is either simply an act of trustful piety without a component of practical politics, or an act of cynical politics without serious attentiveness to Yahwism. Rather, it is exactly a pragmatic act that in good faith is taken to be a Yahwistic intention, deduced from the poetry of Jeremiah, but not in itself recommended by Jeremiah. For that reason, I suggest, the opponents of this view rightly "blame" Baruch, that agent (fictive or not) who let Jeremiah's theocentric utterance touch concrete issues in a decidedly interested way.

Thus I conclude that Baruch and those whom he purportedly represents, that is, the scribal-Deuteronomic circles who enlisted Jeremiah's poetic-Yahwistic discernment for their own purposes, and who likely completed something approximating the canonical process, were, as Carroll proposes, ideologues. We must, however, be precise on what is meant by this label. Carroll uses the term "ideology" in this context as a pejorative term, I believe, in a Marxian sense as "distortion."[24] Moreover, Carroll opposes "rhetoric" to "analysis,"[25] hyperbolic sermon to reality,[26] and experience to ideology,[27] thus suggesting an accent on *willful* distortion.

I do indeed understand what Carroll intends. It may be possible, however, to understand the ideological process of "Baruch" "using" "Jeremiah" as a more dialectical process that does not, in any positivistic way, establish such clear opposition between rhetoric and analysis, sermon and reality, and experience and fact. Marx's study of ideology suggests that God-talk always "reads down" from superstructure to base, from "heaven, religion, and theology" to "earth, law, and politics."[28] Of course, this may be the case, and the opponents of Baruch take such a view. This "lie" is exactly what Marx means when he discusses ideology in terms of distortion.[29]

But if we entertain ideology in Clifford Geertz's more carefully nuanced way, as "making sense" in order to counter the stress of nonsense, we need not drive a wedge between the "religious" and the "real," or in this case between poetry and its "use."[30] We may take as good faith on the part of Baruch the coherence of the two, the poem and its Babylonian "application," so that the critique by the "insolent" in 43:23 is never only against Baruch the pragmatist, but also against Jeremiah the (so to say) "innocent" religionist. In this understanding of ideology, such religious claims are never merely, in Marx's terms, "earth, law, politics," but have a good faith component of "heaven, religion, and theology" as well, which the "insolent" do not want to entertain. That is, the wedge driven between Jeremiah and Baruch by the enemies of Baruch makes it possible to dismiss Baruch as an ideologue who "uses" but does not take seriously the poetic vision of the prophet. Such a dismissive reading, I suggest, is simplistic and excessively cynical, for the interface between serious faith and serious politics is never so one-dimensional. The complexity and intransigence of the public process requires us to give the Baruch party more maneuverability as it moves between poetic truth and political realism.

I suggest that this alternative approach to the ideological factor in the text, not in order to defend or to value Baruch and his ilk but in order to understand the canonical process, is what is evidenced here. If "ideology" moves beyond Jeremiah in a more pragmatic and partisan direction, as is charged by Baruch's opponents, I propose the following. Penultimately, and this will be my main argument, the Baruch community believed passionately in the coherence and identification of Yahweh's intention (which Jeremiah uttered) and Babylonian foreign policy. It is that coherence that gives the words of Jeremiah such usefulness and credibility in the Baruch community, made up as it was of shrewd pragmatics. It is that coherence, between poetry and pragmatic application, that illuminates the place and function of the assaults upon the pro-Egypt party in 43:8-13, 44:1-23, and 44:24-30.

Moreover, as an abrupt and abrasive counterpart to 43:8—44:30, this coherence greatly illumines the placement of chapter 45, the oracle promising a rescue for the person of Baruch.[31] It is Baruch after all—or the party he represents and embodies—who risked, for good-faith as well as pragmatic reasons, support of Jeremiah's rhetoric in the public arena. As Seitz has seen, this oracle in chapter 45 closely parallels 39:15-18, the oracle concerning Ebedmelek, the other case wherein Jeremiah receives public support at great risk. In the oracle concerning Baruch, the countertheme to the well-being of Baruch involves Yahweh's intention to bring "disaster." The great verbs of destruction, "break down and pluck up," are used once more, thus reiterating Yahweh's largest purpose. Thus the oracle of chapter 45 focused on Baruch—or on the Baruch community he represents and embodies—acts as a foil for the larger purpose of the book of Jeremiah, namely, the devastation upon a community of deep disobedience.

The canonical process in the MT tradition, as is well known, has juxtaposed to chapter 45 the Oracles Against the Nations in chapters 46–51. These oracles are rarely studied in canonical context, but they are most often examined for their historical reference points or as a part of the genre of "oracles against the nations." It is to be noticed, however, that in first place among the oracles stands the oracle against Egypt (46:1-28). The Egypt condemned in chapters 43–44, the Egypt taken by Baruch as a counter to Yahweh's intention for Babylon, this Egypt is now in first place for condemnation in the oracles of chapters 46–51. Indeed, in 46:19, it is the "sheltered daughter of Egypt/Memphis" who will be ruined and exiled. Moreover, as the text stands, it is Nebuchadnezzar who will work the devastation (46:13, 26), thus linking the text to 43:10. The culmination of this denunciation of Egypt is a statement of rescue for "Jacob" (46:27-28). Thus, across the canonical sequence of 43:8—44:30, 45:1-5, and 46:1-23, very different genres with different redactional histories, the main point stands: Yahweh's Babylonian policy cannot be resisted. This message coheres with Jeremiah's elusive "foe from the north," and serves Baruch's pragmatic policy.[32] (It will be evident that something is missing in the swift move to the rescue of Judah in 46:27-28, for the primary problem for "Jacob" is not Egypt but Babylon, which at this point still survives in awesome, brutal power.)

I have said, however, that this coherence of Yahweh and Babylon, of theological intention and practical policy, is a *penultimate* coherence treasured by the Baruch community. I use the word *penultimate*, of course, because in 50:1—51:58, at the end of the Oracles Against the Nations, the ultimate judgment is that the alliance between Yahweh and Babylon falls apart, as inevitably it must. In the end, so the text asserts, Yahweh turns against Yahweh's own established ally, Babylon, and destroys it. The reason for such a turn, after such a rhetoric of alliance, is (a) that Yahweh makes no permanent alliances that would permit the absolutizing of any historical structure or institution, and (b) the rhetoric of Jeremiah is characteristically twofold, even if the wording is Deuteronomic; Yahweh not only plucks up and tears down, but plants and builds.[33] There can be, as it now stands, no Jeremiah message that does not make both moves (compare 31:28).

VI

Of course, it is easy enough to say that chapters 50–51 come later from a different group who saw the next historical turn, that is, the move of Cyrus against Babylon (which evoked 2 Isaiah). Even Carroll, however, observes that chapters 50–51 are an exception to the realpolitik of the tradition.[34] This large, relentless judgment about Babylon, against the pro-Babylonian weight of much of the Jeremiah tradition, can indeed be an exception to realpolitik, if we do not begin with a flat, positivistic notion of realpolitik. I propose that the Baruch community—in its "ideology" that is informed by Jeremiah but processed through its own interests, hopes, and fears— never practiced simple realpolitik. (See especially 26:16-19 for something other than realpolitik.) Thus that community, I propose, held together a *penultimate alliance* of Yahweh and Babylon, and an *ultimate confession* that Yahweh has no permanent allies.

Given such a theological norm, albeit not innocent and perhaps not disinterested, this interpretive community could see or anticipate that Yahweh's rule would win out against all pretenders, including a long-standing ally of Yahweh. This conclusion may have been in the service of an interest, but such a nuanced Yahwistic judgment is, I submit, unavoidable in a community in any way serious about Yahwism. This may of course assign to the canonizers too much "theology," which flies in the face of pragmatism. I suggest, however, that this move from the destruction of Egypt in chapter 46 to the destruction of Babylon in chapters 50–51, from the penultimate to the ultimate in this context, is neither simply an act of realpolitik nor simply an abrupt departure from realpolitik, but that this canonizing community was always practicing more than realpolitik. That is, the factoring of Yahweh into the public process is a real and serious move on its part, and not simply disguised code language for interest and preference, as a more positivistic interpretation would insist. The vision of the anguish and buoyancy of the poet made available and even decisive this other "actor" (Yahweh) who is not a pawn of flat political interest.

What is practiced by the Baruch community (which utilizes Jeremiah) is indeed "ideology." I want, however, to follow Fredric Jameson and Paul Ricoeur in their use of Mannheim's category of ideology, twinned as it is with utopia. Ideology in any of its senses—distortion, stress management, or integration—is geared to an intended defense of the status quo. Agreed. But Jameson and Ricoeur, working with Mannheim's categories, have suggested that even the most zealous practitioners of ideology, in this case the community of Baruch, tend to turn ideology beyond itself and spill over into utopia—that is, into a future that is based in a valued status quo, but that runs well beyond that status quo into something richer, even beyond vested interest and beyond present "doable" circumstance. Thus Jameson asserts:

> All class consciousness—or in other words all ideology in the strongest sense, including the most exclusive forms of ruling-class consciousness just as much as that of the oppositional or oppressed classes—is in its very nature Utopian.[35]

If we assume that the Baruch community is in some way the "ruling class" in the exilic period, we may expect, in my judgment, that its hope would move past its protective interest in the status quo.

In like manner, Ricoeur concludes:

> As for myself, I assume completely the inextricable role of this utopian element, because I think that it is ultimately constitutive of any theory of ideology. It is always from the depth of a utopia that we may speak of an ideology.[36]

More recently, Ricoeur has asserted:

> Every society, . . . possesses, or is part of, a sociopolitical imaginaire, that is, an ensemble of symbolic discourses. This imaginaire can function as a rupture or a reaffirmation. As reaffirmation, the imaginaire operates as an "ideology" which can positively repeat and represent the founding discourse of a society, what I call its "foundational symbols," thus preserving its sense of identity. . . . Over against this, there exists the imaginaire of rupture, a discourse of utopia which remains critical of the powers that be out of fidelity to an "elsewhere," to a society that is "not yet." . . . In short, ideology as a symbolic confirmation of the past and utopia as a symbolic opening towards the future are complementary; if cut off from each other they can lead to a form of political pathology.[37]

In our case, it is the "utopia" of Yahweh's ultimate concern for Judah that lies in, with, and under the ideological alliance with Babylonian policy on the part of the Baruch community.

In the case of Jeremiah's canonizers, I submit that in chapters 43–44, 45, and 46, ideology as advocacy of an interest does indeed operate. Finally, only late, in chapters 50–51, ideology pushes beyond itself to daring hope, for God's awaited action. I suggest that this move in chapters 50–51 is not an add-on, not superfluous, not a concession to a tamer faith, but a cogent next move in rhetoric, which may be interested and pragmatic, but never reductionist to the exclusion of the very faith that made the scribes advocates of the large theological vision of Jeremiah.

VII

This move from penultimate Babylonian policy to the ultimate expectation of Babylonian defeat, this move from ideology to utopia, is evidenced in two ways that, in conclusion, I wish to identify. First, the anti-Egypt/pro-Babylon construal of Yahweh's will has run its course by chapter 50. The long poem demolishing the Babylonian empire is capped in the prose "report" of 51:59-64. According to the "report" itself, the functionary to carry out the destruction of Babylon is Seraiah, son of Neraiah, and therefore brother of Baruch.[38] The instigator of the action of Seraiah, however, is none other than Jeremiah. As presented here, the prophet finally turns against Babylon. Jeremiah does two things. He dispatches this voice of the Baruch community; he writes the "disaster" on a scroll that is to be read and instructs the scribe to throw the scroll into the Euphrates, to sink as Babylon will sink.

The substance of Jeremiah's instruction is to announce (and enact?) the end of Babylon, as willed by Yahweh. The actual sequence of words attributed to Jeremiah is more than a little curious. In vv. 61 and 63, instructions are directly given to Seraiah. In v. 62, however, the speech is presented as a reminder to Yahweh. And in v. 64, the first-person verb has no clear subject, though we may infer that the subject is Yahweh. In any case, the intention is clear. The culmination of the book of Jeremiah is the sharp distinction between the plans of Babylon and the intention of Yahweh.[39] (See 29:11 and Isa. 55:8-9 on contrasting "plans.")[40]

What interests us most is the connection of this act of the counter-scroll to the family (and community) of Baruch. In this concluding assertion, the scribal family moves beyond its pragmatic commitment to Babylon and embraces the more radical note of Yahweh's destructive hostility toward Babylon, a hostility that will in time permit Jews to return home from Babylon. The intense ideological commitment that has driven much of this literature is now superseded. That overriding of a provisional commitment may of course be the next step in a larger ideology; it may, however, also be a break with ideology that places the future in the hands of Yahweh, a utopian anticipation beyond the terrible hand of Babylon.[41]

The second variation of this theme of hope beyond ideology I identify in 50:41-42. The long poem against Babylon in chapters 50–51 contains a curious allusion back to 6:22-23, in what is conventionally catalogued as a "Scythian Song."[42] With slight variation, the later poem utilizes the form and wording of the earlier poem. The decisive phrase used in both cases is "no mercy." In the first usage, an unnamed people "from the north" (presumably Babylon) is dispatched by Yahweh in destructive ways against Jerusalem. Such an assertion stands at the center of Jeremiah's dread-filled message. There is coming a threat that will show "no mercy." In the second poem, the same rhetoric is used, again asserting "no mercy," but this time against Babylon (50:43). Thus the canonizers have reused the rhetoric of the prophet, indicating that God's alliance with Babylon is taken as an interim arrangement.[43]

This capacity to hold tentatively but tenuously to a concrete political force, and yet to see that force as deeply problematic, indicates the way in which the scribal canonizers did indeed make use of Jeremiah for their own purposes. Finally, even their political purposes, however, were overcome by the tenacity of a theological vision.

In the end, the fall of Egypt (chapter 46) and the fall of Babylon (chapters 50–51) are, as the book is cast, not simply turns of realpolitik. Nor is this sequence fully comprehended as a statement of vested interest and ideology. In, with, and under the capacity of the scribal community for both realpolitik and ideology, it is Yahweh's sovereignty that prevails and that causes the text to run beyond more managed horizons. That decisive conviction at play in the text reiterates at the end of the canonizing process and the canonical corpus the main claims made at the outset by the "prophet to the nations." The end of the book is, to be sure, a considerable distance from the anguish and wonder of the prophet, for the wildness of the prophet has been toned down. Even at that distance, nonetheless, the interested claims made by the canonizing community of Baruch are not incongruous with the theocentric casting of the public process already at work in the first dangerous utterances that have seeded the larger corpus.[44]

⑤ 5   The Scandal and Liberty of Particularity

IT IS ONLY THE DOMINANT COMMUNITY, OR THOSE ALLIED WITH AND amenable to the dominant community, that does not need to work intensely or intentionally to socialize its young into its vision of reality. Marx surely is correct in his aphorism that "the ideas of the ruling class become the ruling ideas." "The ruling class"—those who govern the imagination, control the flow of images, and adjudicate what is worthy—so much control and legitimate the environment that their young inhale those assumptions and visions without effort. The dominant community nurtures its young into the habits of privilege, certitude, and domination, and the young, wisely and without reflection, receive their inheritance of privilege, certitude, and domination. Thus Peter L. Berger and Thomas Luckmann can readily describe the processes of construction and maintenance, of internalization and externalization, that are essential to the continuity of certain forms of social life.[1] Or to state a beginning point for what follows, adherents to dominant social values and social visions are not likely to trouble about character ethics.

1

In the world of ancient Israel in the period of the Old Testament, it is not difficult to identify the ruling groups whom we may suppose constructed and maintained dominant values. The list of superpowers that dominated the landscape of that ancient world includes, in sequence, Egypt, Assyria, Babylon, and Persia.[2] From an Israelite perspective one can make some differentiations in their several modes of hegemony, so that it appears that Assyria was the most consistently brutal, and that Persia operated in a more benign or enlightened way; but those differences likely were strategic, or at least the Israelite perception and presentation of them are likely strategic. Without fail, the impinging superpower intended to dominate the political landscape, to control military power, and to preempt the authority to tax. The control of military power, moreover, included the right to draft manpower, which issued in forced labor for state projects.

On the whole these concentrations of power tolerated little deviation in matters of importance to them. To ensure compliance, moreover, the political-economic-military power of hegemony is matched, characteristically, with imperial myths and rituals, liturgic activities that legitimated power realities. It is not too much to conclude that the interface of political and liturgical efforts intended to generate a totalizing environment outside of which there were permitted no political forays, and where effective, no deviant imagination. The hegemony maintained both a monopoly of violence and a monopoly of imagination that assured for its own young privilege, certitude, and domination, and that invited into its universal horizon those who stood outside the primary benefits of that monopoly but who had come to terms with that privilege, certitude, and domination that were visible and beyond question.

From an Israelite perspective, the totalizing capacity of hegemony is perceived, characteristically, as arrogant and threatening.[3] Thus with ancient memories of oppression still palpable, Ezekiel can have Pharaoh assert:

> My Nile is my own,
>   I made it for myself. (Ezek. 29:3)

And in the Isaiah tradition, Assyria gloats:

> Has any of the gods of the nations saved their land out of the hand of the king of Assyria? Where are the gods of Hamath and Arpad? Where are the gods of Sepharvaim? Have they delivered Samaria out of my hand? Who among all the gods of these countries have saved their countries out of my hand, that the LORD should save Jerusalem out of my hand? (Isa. 36:18-20)

And Babylon is no different:

> I shall be mistress forever . . .
> I am, and there is no none beside, me . . .
> No one sees me. (Isa. 47:7-10)

We may register only two footnotes to this parade of totalizing superpowers. First, in the early part of the monarchic period in Jerusalem, emerging in a brief pause from imperial interference, the Davidic-Solomonic regime was not beholden to any external power. And yet the evidence we have, admittedly from a certain (Deuteronomic-prophetic) perspective, is that the Jerusalem regime practiced the same totalizing efforts, surely to be "like all the other nations."[4] Both the relentless prophetic critiques and perhaps especially the Rechabite alternative of Jeremiah 35 indicate that even this regime is no exception to the pattern of hegemonic rule.

Second, in addition to the standard lineup of imperial powers, we may mention a prophetic concern about Tyre, especially in Isa. 23:1-18 and Ezekiel 26–28. What interests us is that Tyre's significance is not military and political, but economic. Indeed, Isaiah suggests that Tyre is the epicenter of a world economy that features opulence, self-indulgence, and general social disregard, so that Tyre can be imagined as saying:

> I am a god;
>   I sit in the seat of the gods,
>   in the heart of the seas. (Ezek. 28:2)

This recital of hegemony, focusing on political power but ending with a recognition of commercialism, provides a window on our own current consideration of character ethics. First, I submit that in our time and place the hegemonic power of international corporate capitalism, driven of course by U.S. technological power, creates a totalizing environment that imposes its values, its field of images, its limits of vision, upon all comers. Theodore H. von Laue speaks of *The World Revolution of Westernization,* and more recently Charles Reich terms it "the money government."[5] It is self-evident that this community of ruthless expansionism and those allied with it do not need to use any energy in inculcating their own young into practices of privilege, certitude, and domination. I imagine, moreover, that our modest reflections upon character ethics in such a totalizing environment are not unlike those of Israel in the ancient world, deeply perplexed about how to sustain any vision or practice of life that is not swept away by the force of hegemony. The deep vexation concerns, on the one hand, those of us who live at the center of the hegemony, are implicated in it, and benefit from it. And on the other hand, the deep vexation is also among those in less-privileged places that we are pleased to term "underdeveloped," in wonderment about how to maintain any local, rooted identity in the face of invasive, seemingly irresistible Coca-Cola and inescapable Microsoft.

II

In its relentless imperial matrix, ancient Israel had only a slight chance and thin resources. It is clear, nonetheless, that a central preoccupation of the Old Testament, surely a discernment assembled and transmitted out of a passionate ideological perspective, is to maintain the scandal and liberty of particularity in the face of totalizing threat. I shall suggest that the maintenance of a self-aware, self-conscious alternative identity in the face of totalism is precisely the practice of character ethics that aims to generate and authorize liberated "agents of their own history"; such practice depends upon the great "thickness" of the community that makes possible such liberated agents on a day-to-day basis.

I will organize my efforts around an easy scheme of superpowers: Egypt, Assyria, Babylon, and Persia. (I am of course aware of the historical critical qualifications concerning the literature, but I will deal with the literature in terms of its presentation. For example, texts that deal with the ancient pharaoh of the exodus period will be taken that way without the critical qualification of later dating.)

Israel as an intentional countercommunity practiced relentless, dense memory as an alternative to the co-opting amnesia of the empire.

1. *Concerning Egypt.* It is evident that the Exodus liturgy (Exod. 1–15)

dominates the imagination of Israel and continues to be decisive for Israel's identity. I will mention three aspects of the narrative that pertain to what we may roughly regard as character formation. First, three times, the Passover provisions pay attention to intentional instructing:

> When your children ask you, "What do you mean by this observa-
> tion" . . . ? (Exod. 12:16; compare 13:8, 14)

The liturgy is a launching pad for inculcating conversation. The prescribed response to the child's question is each time a narrative reiteration of a peculiar world with Yahweh at its center.

Second, the entire Passover provision of Exodus 12–13 is quite specific and self-conscious about liturgical detail. It is clear, nonetheless, that the large intention of the narrative and the liturgy is to construct a counter-world whereby Pharaoh's totalizing power and totalizing explanation of reality are regularly defeated. The Israelite boy or girl is invited to live in a social reality where Pharaoh's abusive power does not prevail.

Third, in Exod. 10:1-2, the narrative makes clear that the recital is in order to offer a curriculum for the young:

> Go to Pharaoh; for I have hardened his heart and the heart of his
> officials, in order that I may show these signs [plagues] of mine
> among them, and that you may tell your children and grandchildren
> how I made fools of the Egyptians and what signs I have done
> among them—so that you may know I am the LORD.

The concern—to make this defining memory operative to the third and fourth generations—is crucial for our subject.

2. *Concerning Assyria.* Critical judgment suggests that the book of Deuteronomy is to be understood as an instrument of resistance against Assyrian totalism, perhaps influenced by Assyrian forms of treaty documents.[6] Pivotal to Josiah's reform is the celebration of the Passover (2 Kings 23:21-23). The focus on Passover of course draws resistance to Assyria into the world of Passover resistance to Egypt in Exodus 12–13. It is the disciplined, intentional retelling of the exodus-seder narrative that provides ground for alternative existence outside Assyrian hegemony. The Passover festival recalls Israel's root identity of emancipation and covenant. But it also brings that counteridentity, unendingly contemporary, into the Assyrian crisis.

The regulation of Passover in Deut. 16:1-8 is one of three defining festivals that will give liturgic, dramatic, narrative articulation to Israel's distinctiveness, the other two festivals being Weeks and Booths (16:9-17). Thus the danger and the rescue from Egypt are transposed into an Assyrian world. The provision of 16:1-8 mentions Egypt three times; the following provision for the Festival of Weeks moves more directly to an ethical derivation:

> Rejoice before the LORD . . . you . . . your male and female slaves,
> the Levites resident in your towns, as well as the strangers, the
> orphans, and the widows who are among you. (16:11)

And then the imperative:

> Remember that you were a slave in Egypt. (16:12)

3. *Concerning Babylon.* The great danger for Jewish exiles in Babylon
was assimilation into the totalizing world of Nebuchadnezzar, with the
commensurate abandonment of the particular identity of Judaism. It is
common to recognize that 2 Isaiah is a message to Jews that they will be liberated to go home to Jerusalem. It is my thought, however, that prior to
going home geographically, there must be an emotional, liturgic, imaginative going home to Jewishness. Here I will mention only one text:[8]

> Look to the rock from which you were hewn,
>   and to the quarry from which you were dug.
> Look to Abraham your father
>   and to Sarah who bore you. (Isa. 51:1-2)

I do not follow John Van Seters in his notion that these traditions of the
ancestors were first formulated in the exile.[7] But there is no doubt that the
promissory narratives of Genesis received enormous attention and were
found to be pertinent in this context. It is when all seemed lost in the face
of the totalizing empire that Israel was driven deep into its narrative past, in
order to have an identity apart from the offer of Babylon.

And while there are important historical-critical issues, we may here
mention Daniel 1, wherein the self-aware Jew Daniel negotiates his way
through the civil service of Babylon by a refusal of the rich food of the
empire and a reliance upon the simplicities of a Jewish diet. The refusal of
junk food from the empire is linked to embedment in a particular sense of
identity. The Daniel narrative is an echo of the challenge of exilic Isaiah:

> Ho, everyone who thirsts,
>   come to the waters;
> and you that have no money,
>   come, buy and eat!
> Come, buy wine and milk
>   without money and without price.
> Why do you spend your money for that which is not bread,
>   and your labor for that which does not satisfy? (Isa. 55:1-2)

4. *Concerning Persia.* The issues with Persia are very different, wherein
antagonism has yielded to supportive imperial patronage (Neh. 2:5-8).
Nehemiah operates with the credentials of Persia. Nonetheless, when that
community of Jews engages in an act of reconstitution, the public liturgic
activity is not Persian. It is Torah based, linking Jews to the oldest memories

of Moses (Neh. 8:1-12) and culminating in the Festival of Booths whereby Israel reengages its memory of vulnerability and inexplicable receipt of well-being (Neh. 8:13-18). A primary dimension of "re-boothing" is that the Torah was read for seven consecutive days.

Thus in the face of every empire that sought to comprehend Jewish identity, one can see this community intentionally staking out public, liturgical space to reenact and reclaim its own distinctive identity. That liturgical act is surely an act of faith. It is at the same time an act of resistance, of propaganda, of nurture, whereby the community asserts to its young in direct ways that its existence is not comprehended in the totalizing reality of the empire.

III

As an intentional countercommunity, Israel practiced liberated, imaginative possibility as an alternative to the circumscribed limiting world of imperial administration. A totalizing empire is primarily interested in tax revenues, civil order, and due compliance with imperial expectations and quotas. Such hegemony, however, cannot be sustained unless it is supported by poetic legitimation that seeks to define appropriate social hopes and expectations and inescapable social fears and threats. The empire can never resist seeking control of the emotional life of its subjects, for in emotional life are generated dreams and visions that may be subversive of current order.

Israel, as a community with a peculiar destiny, resisted the preemption of its hopes and fears by imperial confiscation. It did so by maintaining a liturgical, instructional claim that its life was not under the control of the empire but under the governance of the Holy One of Israel who rightly and with great authority denied the effectiveness and legitimacy of imperial claims. Israel's insistence upon such Yahweh-driven possibility is not made on the basis of the "nuts and bolts" of political and economic life, but on the basis of dramatic enactment that refuses to be domesticated by "nuts and bolts." Israel regularly invites its young into a liturgically constructed counterworld of Yahwistic possibility.

1. *Concerning Egypt.* The entire Exodus liturgy serves the sense of Israel's exceptionalism. Yahweh, as a character in a narrative that Egyptian epistemology would never accept, makes possible for the slave community precisely what Pharaoh had declared impossible. The very enactment of the plagues—which make Pharaoh a fool—is the assertion that there is emancipating power at work beyond the reach of Pharaoh.

More than that, the liturgy is replete with the protection of Israel, singled out from the massive destruction of the empire:

> Thus I will make a distinction between my people and your people.
> (Exod. 8:23)

> All the livestock of the Egyptians died, but of the livestock of the Israelites not one died. (Exod. 9:6)

> The hail struck down everything. . . . Only in the land of Goshen, where the Israelites were, there was no hail. (Exod. 9:25-26)

> There will be a loud cry throughout the whole land of Egypt. . . . But not a dog shall growl at any of the Israelites . . . so that you may know that the LORD makes a distinction between Egypt and Israel. (Exod. 11:6-7)

There are matters possible for Israel that Pharaoh would never permit.

2. *Concerning Assyria.* The linkage between liturgic reconstrual and a radical alternative ethic is most clear in Deut. 15:1-18, which places next to Passover the year of release, whereby Israel resists the emergence of a permanent interclass. Both Jeffries M. Hamilton and Moshe Weinfeld have suggested that this Torah provision is the quintessential mark of Israel's distinctive ethic.[9] The practice of debt cancellation stands in deep opposition to the imperial economy, which is a practice of hierarchical power and social stratification. This provision stands at the center of Deuteronomy, a script designed to distinguish Israel from Assyrian possibility.

I cite this provision at this point because it is not simply a legal regulation. It is rather a remarkable exploration of a social possibility that is clearly unthinkable in the empire. The empire stands or falls with the administration of debt, for it is debt that distinguishes between the powerful and the have-nots.[10]

Deuteronomic resistance to Assyrian impingement, however, is not simply liturgical. It is also the dreaming vision of an alternative economy that imagines neighbors living with generous, palpable concern for each other. And the energy for such subversive activity is, predictably, grounded in memory:

> Remember that you were slaves in the land of Egypt; the LORD redeemed you; for this reason I lay this command upon you today. (Deut. 15:15)

Assyria or any other empire would regard this social posture as impossible because Assyria has, as yet, no exodus memory.

3. *Concerning Babylon.* The challenge of 2 Isaiah is to create imaginative space for Jewishness. The danger is that Israel in exile will give everything over to Babylonian definitions of the possible. So the assertion:

> My thoughts are not your thoughts,
>   nor are your ways my ways, says the LORD. (Isa. 55:8)

I suggest that this assertion is not a generic invitation to repent of sin; it is rather a concrete assault on Jewish readiness to accept Babylonian definitions of the possible. Yahweh has another way, another thought, another possibility. Babylon offered food that is not bread, and labor that does not satisfy, but Yahweh offers wine and milk and bread without money and without price (Isa. 55:1-2). Babylon thought to keep everything frozen and everyone in place to perpetuity. But Yahweh anticipates in exultation:

> You shall go out in joy
>   and be led back in peace. (Isa. 55:12)

Babylon had become an arena for abandonment and the absence of God. But now Yahweh asserts:

> With great compassion I will gather you. . . .
> With everlasting love I will have compassion on you.
> (Isa. 54:7-8)

The world that 2 Isaiah imagines is not a world from which Yahweh has been forcibly eliminated. Yahweh is still there. For that reason, Babylonian designations of reality are not finally effective.

4. *Concerning Persia*. The relation between Israel and Persia is different from Israel's relation to previous hegemonic powers. And yet, even with Persia the Jews knew their lives were deeply circumscribed by imperial pressures and realities. This sense of limitation and pressure is evidenced in the great prayer of Ezra in Nehemiah 9. The prayer moves between Israel's wickedness and God's mercy. The final petition, however, lets us see, beyond the intensity between Yahweh and Israel, this third party:

> Here we are, slaves to this day—slaves in the land that you gave to
> our ancestors to enjoy its fruit and its good gifts. Its rich yield goes
> to the kings whom you have set over us because of our sins; they
> have power also over our bodies and over our livestock at their
> pleasure, and we are in great distress. (Neh. 9:36-37)

The reality of restriction is evident. The text nonetheless suggests two facets of emancipated possibility that remained outside Persian administration. The first of these is an act of imagination in the form of prayer. The prayer is a bid for reality that lies beyond the control of Persia, a bid that shows this intentional community not yet conceding everything to hegemony. The second is that the prayer is followed in 9:38—10:39 by a solemn community covenant in which the leaders of the community vow to act in solidarity concerning economic matters, a solidarity that echoes the old year of release.

The text is saturated with communal, liturgic, imaginative practice in which a zone of social possibility, rooted in Yahweh, outside imperial regimentation, is maintained, celebrated, practiced, and made visible.

IV

Israel as an intentional countercommunity gave articulation to a covenantal ethic of neighborliness as an alternative to the commoditization of social relationships it sensed in imperial practice. I do not want to overemphasize the ethical, as it seems to me the liturgic-imaginative effort to create and protect alternative space is more important. Israel, however, cannot entertain or imagine alternative human space, sponsored as it is by Yahweh, except space that is saturated with ethical urgency, ethical possibility, and ethical requirement. Indeed it is the practice of Torah obedience to the rooted claims of the community that is the instrument and guarantee of liberated life beyond imperial reductionism:

> I will keep your law continually,
>> forever and ever.
> I shall walk at liberty,
>> for I have sought your precepts.
> I will speak of your decrees before kings,
>> and shall not be put to shame. (Ps. 119:44-46)

1. *Concerning Egypt.* As the exodus narrative is the paradigmatic assertion of community beyond the reality of totalizing power, so the Sinai recital is the paradigmatic articulation of neighborly ethics that counters the ethic of Pharaoh. In its completed tradition, Israel understood that emancipation from Egypt was not for autonomy, but was to the counterservice of Yahweh. And while we may focus on a variety of commands that epitomize that alternative ethic rooted in liturgy, we may settle for the first command: no other gods except Yahweh the God of the exodus who delegitimizes every other loyalty. While the commands of Sinai are demanding and abrasive, they would never be confused with Pharaoh's commands, for they are in general aimed at a communitarianism that makes "hard labor" impossible.[11]

The linkage between the holiness of Yahweh and the concreteness of neighborliness is wondrously voiced in Deut. 10:17-19:

> For the LORD your God is god of gods and Lord of lords, the great God, mighty and awesome, who is not partial and takes no bribe, who executes justice for the orphan and the widow, and who loves the strangers, providing them food and clothing. You shall also love the stranger, for you were strangers in the land of Egypt.

It is precisely the God who commands lords, gods, and pharaohs who loves immigrants and displaced persons and who provides them food and clothing. This ethic arises from the memory and from the possibility of an alternative to Pharaoh.

2. *Concerning Assyria.* Deuteronomy as a contrast program makes one of its foci "widows and orphans," that is, the paradigmatic powerless and

vulnerable in society. The Israelite ethic urged here, alternative to imperial rapaciousness, is precisely concerned for those without resources or leverage to maintain and protect themselves:

> Every third year you shall bring out the full tithe of your produce for that year, and store it within your towns; the Levites, because they have no allotments or inheritance with you, as well as the resident aliens, the orphans and the widows in your towns may come and eat their fill. (Deut. 14:28-29; compare 16:11, 14; 24:17, 19-21; 26:12-13)

This social horizon, moreover, is rooted in exodus memories:

> Remember that you were a slave in Egypt, and diligently observe these statues. (Deut. 16:12; compare 24:18, 22)

Against Assyrian amnesia, which permits exploitative neighborly relations, it is precisely narrative embedment in the Exodus tradition that energizes the radical economics of Deuteronomy.

3. *Concerning Babylon.* The vision of 2 Isaiah, rooted in exodus imagery, only in a general way understood Israel's life to be a practice of justice (42:1-4), light (42:6; 49:6), and covenant (42:6; 49:8), a general way that envisioned a differently ordered economy. We may, however, insist that in 3 Isaiah, albeit beyond the Babylonian period, the visionary ethics of 2 Isaiah continued to ferment and evoke ferocious dispute in the community concerning ethical possibility. Thus in Isa. 56:2-8, a powerful urging for inclusiveness is voiced, and in 58:6-7, the quintessence of covenantalism is voiced as a precondition for Yahweh's presence in the community:

> Is not this the fast that I choose:
> > to loose the bonds of injustice,
> > to undo the thongs of the yoke,
> to let the oppressed go free,
> > and to break every yoke?
> Is it not to share your bread with the hungry,
> > and bring the homeless poor into your house;
> when you see the naked, to cover them,
> > and not to hide yourself from your own kin? (Isa. 58:6-7)

This issue of inclusiveness is not easily settled in the years immediately after the exile. What is clear, nonetheless, is that the peculiar social vision of Israel continued to summon and empower, even when the community had limited resources and feared for its own survival.

4. *Concerning Persia.* The lyrical anticipations of the Isaiah tradition came to concrete implementation in the reform of Nehemiah. Though authorized by the Persians, it is clear that Nehemiah and Ezra, in the recon-

stitution of an intentional community of Torah, had to struggle mightily for a neighborly ethic rooted in Israel's peculiar tradition.

Most spectacularly, in Neh. 5, Nehemiah addresses the economic crisis whereby some Jews were exploiting other Jews in a way that created a permanent underclass.[12] Nehemiah's demanding alternative vision is rooted in the exodus memory, alludes to the old Torah, is aware of Israel's distinctiveness, and requires concrete, costly economic decisions:

> As far as we were able, we have bought back our Jewish kindred who been sold to other nations. The thing you are doing is not good. Should you not walk in the fear of our God, to prevent the taunts of the nations our enemies? . . . Let us stop this taking of interest. Restore to them this very day, their fields, their vineyards, their olive orchards, and their houses, and the interest on money, grain, wine, and oil that you have been exacting from them. (Neh. 5:8-11)

In every imperial context, Israel's peculiar ethic is kept alive, each time rooted in old liturgical memory, but each time brought to bear upon concrete social history in a way that requires the covenant community to act peculiarly against the common definitions of imperial social reality.

V

I want now to reflect in three ways upon this sequencing of *memory, possibility,* and *ethic* through the several imperial hegemonies that ancient Israel lived with.

1. The practice of an ethic rooted in *an intentional particular communal narrative* suggests a community characteristically at risk in the face of a seemingly irresistible imperial pressure toward homogenization. The pressure of triage, of the elimination of surplus people, worked massively against the Israelites, if not in terms of physical violence, then through ideological violence that sought always to eradicate Israel's sense of itself and sense of Yahweh's reality.[13] I think it impossible to overstate the enduringly ominous threat of elimination which required a liturgy, a socialization, and an ethic that had to be understood as resistance.

(a) This resistance *pertains to Jewishness* in a most concrete sense, for which I will cite two instances in the long history of marginality. The Maccabean revolt against Roman homogenization in the second century B.C.E. is of course a pivot point for the intertestamental period. Roman triage was not directly violent, but it was determined to eliminate Jewish oddness. The only point upon which I comment is the brief notation in 1 Macc. 1:11-15 that "renegade Jews" sought a covenant with the Gentiles:

> They built a sports-stadium in the Gentile style in Jerusalem, they removed the marks of circumcision and repudiated the Holy Covenant. They intermarried with Gentiles and abandoned themselves to evil ways.[14]

The pressure of a "universal identity" is always a threat to a particular identity, so that assimilation is ever a clear and present danger.

That pressure of homogeneity and threat of triage by assimilation was directly asserted in an ad in the *New York Times* in the form of a litany that made this urging:

> We prayed for Israel when its survival was threatened in
> 1967 and 1973.
> Our prayers were answered.
> We prayed for the redemption of Soviet Jewry during the
> dark years of Communism.
> Our prayers were answered.
> We prayed for the release of Syrian Jewry, hostages to a
> most aggressive regime.
> Our prayers were answered.
> Now it is time to recite a prayer for ourselves—
> an embattled American Jewry. . . . Our birthrate is too low
> and our rate of intermarriage too high. The real question is
> will we survive?[15]

I make no judgment about this ad or about its ideology. I note it to say that the issue of a distinct community of character is a recurring one among the heirs of ancient Israel.

(b) Our concern here, however, more likely concerns *the distinctive ethic of the Christian church*. The end of Christendom in Western Europe and in the United States is likely a good. It is obvious that the church in the United States is not in a position parallel to that of ancient Israel in the empire or to the exposure of current Judaism. It is evident nonetheless that what might have passed for a "Christian ethic" in Christendom has now been thoroughly permeated by secularism in both liberal and conservative modes. And therefore attentiveness to peculiar narrative identity seems to me an urgent practical enterprise in a religious community so bland as to lose its raison d'être. The problematic is to practice a peculiar identity that is not craven in its frightened moralism of the right or the left.

(c) An ethic of resistance—regularly needed in ancient Israel, needed now in my judgment in a depositioned church in the West—is urgent now in a different way in the face of the power of corporate capitalism, supported as it is by military and technological power in the westernization of the world. Around the globe, *local communities with peculiar identities and destinies* are profoundly under threat from "the money government" that has no patience with or regard for rooted communities. Thus the issue of ideological triage and the capacity for locally rooted resistance is not singularly a Jewish or a church question, but it is a question for the shape and viability of humanness in a drastically reorganized world. I suggest that for Christians and Jews who are situated in and are beneficiaries of the expanding world economy, attentiveness to, appreciation for, and support of local resistance—which may take many forms—is an issue of paramount importance.

2. Because I have framed my discussion in terms of *local resistance* to *universalizing pressures*, a framing I think unavoidable in the Old Testament, the question that must be asked is this: is such an approach inevitably sectarian, concerned with funding and authorizing a separatist community? In the first instant, I suspect that this approach to ethics is inevitably aimed at the particularity of the community. And certainly the primary force of the Old Testament is the assertion and maintenance of the distinctive community of Israel. Moreover, I believe that a particularistic ethic of resistance is now urgent in light of the massive power of the "Coca-Cola–izing" of the world.

Having acknowledged that much, two important qualifications are in order. First, Israel over time did not live in a cultural, liturgic vacuum. It was endlessly engaged in interaction with other cultures, and regularly appropriated from the very forces it intended to critique and resist, so that the materials for this distinctive ethic in the sixth century are very different from what purports to be thirteenth-century resistance. The process of deciding what to appropriate (and how) in the midst of resistance is completely hidden from us. The dual process of resistance and appropriation is unmistakable. Thus, for example, Hosea seems to mount a polemic against "fertility religion," but does so by Yahwistic appeal to the modes and images of fertility religion.[16]

Second, while it is not primary, it is evident that Israel's distinctive identity and ethic are an offer, summons, and invitation to the world around it (that is the imperial world) to share its neighbor ethic. While the texts characteristically focus on immediate concrete crises, it is equally clear that Israel's long-term hope is that the "impossible possibility" of covenant, rooted in the creator's practice of steadfast love and justice, can and will be enacted everywhere. Characteristically, Israel believes and trusts that an antineighbor ethic cannot prevail, and that the gods who legitimate such an ethic will be defeated. Israel understands itself at Sinai to be at the edge of Yahweh's coming rule, which will indeed reach to the ends of the earth, so that kings and princes will end their futility and join in doxological obedience, the very doxological obedience that is definitional for Israel's life. At its best (but not always), this deep hope is free from Israel's own ideological benefit. That is, the coming rule is a rule of Yahweh and not a rule of preference for Israel.

3. I conclude with a reference to Jacob Neusner. In his study of Jewish

ritual practice, Neusner judges that the stylized gestures and words of ritual are aids in the daily work of being "Jews through the power of our imagination."[17] Indeed, Neusner opines that Jewishness is hazardous and venturesome enough that it requires a daily act of imagination, without which there would not be Jews.

Mutatis mutandis, I propose that in Christendom Christians needed no such effort, for identity came—as it always does for dominant faith—simply with the territory. The depositioning of Christian faith in the West, however, makes the community of the baptized a community now more fully dependent upon daily acts of imagination for the maintenance of identity. The daily acts evoking Christian identity are likely to be ethical as well as liturgic. The beginning point is the recognition that serious identity is not a cultural given, as in former times of domination, but now is an oddness requiring courageous intentionality.

6 Always in the Shadow of the Empire

THE COMMUNITY OF FAITH, OF COURSE, NEVER LIVES IN A VACUUM. IT IS always in the midst of cultural reality, which is thick and dense and powerful. As Richard Niebuhr has made clear in his classic study, the relationship between cultural reality and a community of baptismal faith is endlessly unsettled, problematic, and under negotiation.[1]

The reasons why our time is now commonly judged to be a season of tension are not difficult to detect. It seems evident that *technological individualism* coupled with *unlimited and unbridled corporate power and corporate wealth* that appear to be beyond the governance of nation-states has created a set of cultural values that are aggressively antihuman.[2] There are times when church and cultural context can live in some kind of mutuality; but this is not one of those times, for gospel rootage requires resistance to such aggressive antihumanism. Such resistance in turn requires great intentionality, embodied in concrete disciplines of body, mind, and heart. For without such disciplines, it is evident that the church community will either be massaged and seduced until it is co-opted, or it will end in the powerlessness of despair.

My own field of study and reflection is the Old Testament. For that reason, in what follows I will explore some of the ways in which the Israelite faith community practiced its intentionality as a community called and mandated by a God with quite peculiar purposes in the world.

Only the most naive reading of the Old Testament can imagine that ancient Israel was a sweet, serene religious community of pure motives. Any alert reading makes clear that Israel was endlessly conflicted. Much of the conflict, moreover, concerns ways of relating to the cultural environment in which it was embedded. It is unmistakable that ancient Israel had a rich, ongoing, variegated interaction with its cultural environment, oftentimes being imposed upon by that environment, sometimes being coerced to accommodate, and sometimes willingly appropriating from its environment. In sum, it is plausible to suggest that the *actual practice* of Israel was largely synergistic. That is, Israel was not so different from other peoples and freely adapted and adopted, likely in quite pragmatic ways. Over against that actual practice, however, the Old Testament itself is likely written from *a distinct, self-conscious theological-ideological perspective*. That perspective challenged the actual practice of synergism (syncretism) and championed the practice of distinctiveness that is rooted in distinctive disciplines and expressed in distinctive ethical consequences.[3] It is no easy matter to assess the relationship between common practice and self-conscious perspective, for they no doubt overlap as well as stand in tension. For our purposes, however, we may attend primarily to the theological-ideological perspective of distinctiveness, for it is here that we arrive at the closest parallels to our own resolve to resist aggressive antihumanism by a countercultural approach.

The relationship between Israelite faith and an environment that variously nourishes, empowers, distorts, and opposes is an ongoing one of incredible density. I propose, however, that one available way to consider this tension and interaction over time is to organize our reflections around the several empires that in rough sequence dominated Israel's public life. These several empires had proximately different policies and attitudes toward subjugated peoples. Consequently Israel's response, in each case, is commensurately different. But in all of these cases, we can learn of Israel's characteristic resolve to maintain its distinct identity and to protect space for its liberated imagination and, consequently, for its distinctive covenantal ethic. The maintenance of distinctive identity and the protection of space for distinctive imagination and ethic takes some intentional doing. Israel's achievement in this regard is at best mixed. It is clear, nonetheless, that it did try.

1

Israel is an intentional, distinctive community in the world dominated by Egypt. Life lived under Egyptian hegemony was surely inevitable, given geopolitical reality. Even as Egypt constitutes the most stable reference point for the foreign policy of contemporary Israel, so in the ancient world Egypt occupied the southern end of the Fertile Crescent and was in every season a force in the life of Israel. Egypt, moreover, had as a constant of its foreign policy the effort to claim the area of Palestine for its own sphere of influence, in order to create a buffer zone against the various formidable powers to the north.

There can be little doubt that Egypt was a constant pressure upon the community of Israel all through the biblical period. That geohistorical reality, however, is transformed in the Old Testament so that Egypt is not simply one of several such impinging powers. Rather, Egypt takes on paradigmatic significance in the imagination of Israel. Thus Egypt is portrayed as the quintessential oppressive power, and Pharaoh is rendered as a representative rival to the authority of Yahweh. Thus the socioeconomic reality of Egypt takes on mythic proportion. This preoccupation, always fed by concrete reality, is especially evident in the liturgical account of the exodus in chapters 1–15, which concerns the thirteenth-century clash in the time of Moses and the incessant meddling of Egypt in Judean matters in the sixth century.[4] The latter in turn produced both the tradition of Jeremiah (43–44) that a return to Egypt gives closure to the story of faith begun with

Exodus, and the tradition of Ezekiel, which critiques Egypt for its arrogant defiance of Yahweh (Ezek. 29–32).

In the memory of Israel, the ancestral narratives of Genesis are framed in the beginning by an acknowledgment in Gen. 12:12-20 that Egypt has a monopoly of food in the ancient world, and at the end by an account of the actions of Joseph, progenitor of Israel, who aids and abets Pharaoh's monopoly of food in a way that reduces the agricultural population to debt-slavery (Gen. 47:13-26). Thus Egypt is presented as a source of life for Israel, but also as an aggressive agent, which enslaves those who seek its resources for life. Much of Israelite imagination consists in coming to terms with the catch-22 of food and bondage, or conversely, no-bondage/no-food.

There can be no doubt, moreover, that pharaonic notions of exploitation, which fated individual persons to be submerged in and for state purposes, operated in Israel. Thus Pharaoh is reported to be father-in-law to Solomon (1 Kings 3:1), and Solomon's policy of forced labor echoes Egyptian practices. In Egypt's own imperial practice and in the derivative practice of Solomon within Israel, the threat against Israel's distinctiveness has a socio-economic, political cast. The social practices enacted in the name of Egyptian gods are deeply antihuman, and in Israel's purview anti-Yahwistic, for the peculiar God of Israel intended a human community that does not exploit. The resistance Israel is to practice against this alien ideology that legitimates alien social practice is as paradigmatic as is the role of Pharaoh. That is, the way in which Israel resists Egypt is the characteristic way in which Israel will subsequently resist every aggressor empire.

We may identify *two disciplines of resistance* that mark the life of Israel in its relation to Egypt. The resistance Israel practices vis-à-vis Egypt is rooted in the most elemental conviction that Yahweh wills otherwise. Yahweh wills otherwise to the state building project that monopolizes labor power. Yahweh wills otherwise to surplus wealth, whereby some live indulgently from the produce of others. Yahweh wills otherwise than exploitative oppression. Yahweh wills otherwise than the Egyptian socio-theological system. Yahweh engages in counteractivity, and therefore Israel, as subject of Yahweh, must resist.

Israel develops and practices *liturgical resistance* by a stylized, regularly enacted drama whereby Egyptian power is given liturgical articulation and Israel is invited—through the course of the drama—to move outside Egyptian hegemony to its own distinctive practice of life.

The substance of Israel's resistance is through the regular reenactment of the Exodus liturgy of Exodus 1–15, which is presented to us as a historical narrative. Each time, over the generations, that Israel participated in this drama of counterreality, Israel imagined and construed a social world outside the hegemonic control of Pharaoh. Indeed, the very doing of the drama itself permitted emancipated imagination that refused the definitions of reality sponsored by Egypt.

The liturgy provides a script for a season of counterbehavior.[5] The first aspect of counterbehavior is *the public voicing of pain:*

> The Israelites groaned under their slavery, and cried out. Out of the slavery their cry for help rose up to God. God heard their groaning, and God remembered his covenant with Abraham, Isaac, and Jacob. God looked upon the Israelites, and God took notice of them. (Exod. 2:23-25)

The world of Pharaoh produced great pain, but it was silenced pain in which brick-producing slaves were to accept their suffering and abuse as appropriate to their condition. The public voicing of pain is the refusal to accept suffering in docility, and to resist the status of slave and the abuse that comes with that status. The very first utterance in the liturgy makes available that which Egypt forcibly denied.

Second, this liturgy dares to offer *a critique that ridicules established power.* Obviously such actions are precluded in the empire, for the maintenance of illicit power depends upon the stifling of dissent. The long recital of the plague narrative (Exod. 7–11), however, is shot through with mockery whereby Yahweh "makes sport" of Pharaoh and thereby erodes that authority (compare 10:1-2). The critique includes the assertion that Egypt "could not," that is, had reached the end of its technological capacity (Exod. 8:18), the futile attempts at deceptive bargaining that seek to deceive Moses (8:25; 10:8-10, 24), and the final, pitiful capitulation of Pharaoh who slowly and progressively must concede everything to Yahweh (12:32). This liturgy is a scenario of reality that contradicts Egyptian reality. This distinctive community is invited to affirm that *the world constructed in liturgy* is more reliable and more credible than the world "out there." The purpose of such liturgy is to nurture imagination and to equip Israel with the nerve to act out of its distinctiveness in the face of formidable, hostile power.

Third, the payoff of such daring imagination is the dance and song of the women, enacted as a gesture of defiance:

> Sing to the *Lord,* for he has triumphed gloriously;
> horse and rider he has thrown into the sea. (Exod. 15:21)

It is clear that this liturgical act—liturgical dance?!—is an act of unadministered, unauthorized freedom whereby the erstwhile slaves give bodily expression to their freedom, the very freedom of bodies Pharaoh could not permit.

The very process of liturgy thus creates an environment and a community that understands itself to be special, under a special mandate of emancipation from that Holy Power that Pharaoh cannot withstand. There can be little doubt that intentional resistance is rooted in the imagination and maintenance of an alternative world in which ostensive powers of intimidation are narratively discredited and dethroned.

The form of the liturgy is detailed in Exod. 12–13 in the provisions for

Passover. We do not know about the actual "history" of the Passover festival. What we do know is that Passover emerged, is situated in the text, and is regarded in Israel as the occasion and script for the periodic, disciplined, intentional reenactment and replication of the exodus narrative. It is the cultic staging whereby in every circumstance, through every generation, this community sustains and makes visible and unavoidable a distinctive identity of emancipation and of resistance to the pressures of pharaonic culture.

We may identify three facets of this form of reapplication. First, it includes detailed, carefully observed bodily gestures—concerning specific foods prepared in specific ways and markings of blood on doorposts as a visible announcement of protective inscrutability in this community not subject to pharaonic administration. These sacramental acts deny the legitimacy of the brute power of Pharaoh. Second, along with bodily, sacramental gesture, there is prescribed wording designed to inculcate the young and to socialize them into this perception of reality. It is abundantly clear that the adults who preside over and reiterate the wording understand it to be a political act of emancipation and resistance always again to be undertaken:

> When your children ask you, "What do you mean by this observance?" you shall say, "It is the passover sacrifice to the LORD for he passed over the houses of the Israelites in Egypt when he struck down the Egyptians but spared our houses." And the people bowed their heads and worshiped. (Exod. 12:27)

This community does not flinch from the violence of these founding narratives, the violence enacted by Yahweh on their behalf. It does not, moreover, blink at the claim of oddness and privilege in the eyes of Yahweh, a privilege never granted to them by pharaonic power.

Third, the provisions for Passover make clear that this is a theological-ideological act not contained in ethnic boundaries:

> Any slave who has been purchased may eat of it after he has been circumcised. . . . If an alien who resides with you wants to celebrate the passover to the LORD, all his males shall be circumcised; then he may draw near to celebrate it . . . there shall be one law for the native and for the alien who resides among you. (Exod. 12:44-49)

The offer is inclusive. But it is not casual. One must be prepared to accept a costly mark to qualify for this community of emancipation and resistance.

Along with liturgical reiteration, this community accepted *rigorous disciplines* for the sake of alternative community. These disciplines we regularly call *commandments* or even *laws*. The emancipating, resisting community, in the imagination of its self-presentation, moved along to Sinai.[6] Mount Sinai, in this tradition, is *the mountain of address*. There Israel heard the very voice of Yahweh (Exod. 20:1-17), and then they heard the mediation of Yahweh in the voice of Moses (vv. 18-21). In this holy voice and in its Mosaic echo, it heard a voice of summons and of assurance, a voice of demand and of promise, a voice guaranteeing a peculiar identity. And there they listened. Thus emerges the verb *shema'* as the defining claim of Israel's life. In listening, Israel knows itself not to be self-made, self-invented, or self-imagined. In that listening, moreover, Israel knows it must cease to listen to the voice of Pharaoh that defines reality in terms of brick quotas. In listening, Israel comes to the startling, dangerous conviction that its life consists not in bricks for the empire, but in acts of neighborliness whereby Israel replicates Exodus for its neighbors.

The Sinai address of command is complex and varied, and often contradictory. I will mention only two commands, epitomize the best of Israel's counterpractice, while acknowledging there is much else that is not so noble.[7] First, there stands at the center of Torah commands the practice of sabbath, the steady practice of work stoppage that makes visible the claim that life consists in being and not in doing or having. I have no doubt that the recovery of this discipline is decisive for the reenactment of this community of emancipation and resistance.[8] Second, the first specific law in the Sinai utterances after the decalogue, given in Exod. 21:1-11, concerns "the year of release," whereby Israel is enjoined to engage in a countereconomics that willingly cancels the debts of neighbors and permits the indebted to rejoin the economy as a full and viable partner. It is this neighborly act of debt cancellation that is the taproot of all Jewish and Christian notions of forgiveness.[9] Forgiveness is cancellation of debts in every zone of existence; this countercommunity takes as its foremost social characteristic the refusal to exploit the poor, the refusal to get even, the refusal to hold grudges, the refusal to exact vengeance. All of these practices, to be sure, are at the core of the pharaonic enterprise, but Yahweh authorizes and summons otherwise.

Israel knows that Egypt is endlessly resolved, vigilant, and canny for its way of life. In the narrative of counterreality, however, it becomes clear—over and over in reenactment—that the Egyptian project is doomed. In the end, Pharaoh is desperate and must say to Moses, "Bless me!" (Exod. 12:32).[10] In the end the repressive achievements of Pharaoh are empty. This little community that begins in pain and ends in dancing, that stops its life for sabbath, that cancels debts for the sake of neighborliness, in the end this community has in its midst the force for life, and is the wave of the future. It is so because in the end, Yahweh denies Pharaoh any authority, even over Egypt (compare Exod. 19:5: "The whole earth is mine.").

11

Israel is an intentional, distinctive community in the world dominated by Assyria. The rise of Assyrian power with Tiglath-Pileser III in 745 created a new culture of domination that pressured Israel and Judah for a century until the fall of Ashurbanipal in 627 and the destruction of Nineveh in 612. The Assyrians were a most formidable power, at one point extending their hegemony even into Egypt. They were also, in their own annals, portrayed as uncommonly cruel and brutalizing. In response to the formidable and intimidating power of Assyria, Israelite and Judean kings were wont to give in and accept Assyrian definitions of reality.

It is clear, nonetheless, that there was maintained in Judah an insistent alternative to Assyrian hegemony, an alternative endlessly reiterating the claim that Judah's *sure future* could be based only upon loyalty to Yahweh, the emancipating, commanding God, and consequently in resistance to Assyrian hegemony. I will mention three literary evidences of this alternative identity. First, the prophet Isaiah offers in most magisterial form an alternative vision of reality. He does not so much address the ethical detail of Judah's life, but rather focuses on the larger issue of competing political-theological loyalties. Isaiah endlessly reiterates that Judah must *trust* in Yahweh, who governs history and who will guarantee Judah in the face of imperial threat.

We know very little about the tactical ways of prophetic utterance in Israel. What is unmistakable, however, is that the prophet endlessly invites Israel to an alternative imaginative scenario of reality, wherein Assyria is denied domination and Yahweh is shown to be an adequate guarantee of life. Thus in the well-known word play of 7:9, in a bid for loyalty to the world construed around Yahweh, the prophet asserts:

> If you do not stand firm in faith,
> you shall not stand at all.

In the Isaiah tradition, faith is engagement with all of the distinctive practices of covenant, most particularly the practice of justice and righteousness (compare 5:7).

The alternative of *unfaith* is to abandon the defining marks of Yahwism, and to embrace the world of anxiety, collusion, and self-indulgence authorized and defined by Assyria. Indeed, the prophet is reductionist in insisting that these are the only two options.

The same poignant contrast is voiced in Isa. 8:5-8:

> Because this people has refused the waters of Shiloh (*shalom*) that flow gently, and melt in fear . . . therefore the Lord is bringing up against it the mighty flood waters of the River, the king of Assyria and all his glory; it will rise above all its channels and overflow its banks; it will sweep into Judah as a flood, and pouring over it, it will reach up to the neck.

The poet uses the metaphor of *gentle waters* (Yahwism) and *raging waters* (Assyria) as the only alternatives available. Here the poet does not enumerate the disciplines of Yahwism (compare 1:16-17), but surely alludes to the Sinai requirements of loving God in holiness and loving neighbor in justice.

This contrasting image culminates:

> And its outspread wings will fill the breadth of your land, O Immanuel. (8:8)

The address to "Immanuel" is ironic. It alludes to the abiding promises made to the house of David, only to announce that the throne of David is precarious and will be overwhelmed:

> No faith . . . no standing,
> no obedience . . . no promise.

Except that the Isaiah tradition cannot ever leave it there, for the Davidic-Immanuel imagery is endlessly resilient for Isaiah. In the very next chapter, the scion of David is celebrated:

> There will be endless peace
> for the throne of David and his kingdom.
> He will establish and uphold it
> with justice and with righteousness
> from this time onward and forevermore. (9:7)

Judah is warned and threatened about Assyrian definitions of reality. In the end, however, Assyria is no match for Yahweh's promises to David.

Micah was a sometime contemporary of Isaiah and, in a different way, makes the same affirmations. First, of the texts I will mention, the poet castigates the greedy who "covet fields and seize houses" (2:2).[11] The ones who violate Yahwism's covenantalism in such a way will lose out when the land is redivided, perhaps by the Assyrians (v. 4). Thus the expectations of Yahweh that will secure the community concern economic covenantalism in which the claims of the neighbor are not disregarded. Judah as a "contrast society" is premised on the elemental command, "Thou shalt not covet," which is here understood as broad social policy and practice.

The devastating warning that such coveting will bring disaster is matched in the Micah tradition by two assurances. In 5:2-6, it is anticipated that a new governing authority will reestablish Judah and give peace and security (5:4) and, if necessary, will defeat Assyria and occupy the land. In the end, however, what is envisioned is not simply the defeat of the empire, but a great scenario of reconciliation, in which "peoples and nations" will submit to Yahweh's Torah in Zion and will decide for disarmament and peace (4:1-4; compare Isa. 2:1-5). What is so remarkable is that the commitment to *Torah* and to *peace* is a peculiar vision of Judah against the military inclination of the empire. In the imaginings of the poet, however, the peaceable

Torah vision of Israel prevails, so that the "contrast community" of Yahweh offers the model and option eventually embraced by all nations. The Micah vision bespeaks the deep resolve and resilience of this alternative. Holding to the vision itself is a discipline and a mark of this community, a long-term refusal to give in to a more accommodating but hopeless social practice.

Third, it is plausible that Deuteronomy, the most intentional theological ecclesiology in the Old Testament, is offered as a contrast to Assyrian power. In its fictive articulation, Deuteronomy assaults the "Canaanites." Common scholarly judgment, however, regards Deuteronomy as an eighth/seventh-century document, so that "the Canaanites" are stand-ins for the Assyrians, the central power of the time that sought to erode Israelite nerve and insinuate Assyrian claims into Israel's imagination.[12] (See the scornful attempts in Isa. 36:4-10, 36:13-20, 37:8-13.)

It is widely recognized that covenant receives its definitive voicing in Deuteronomy, the covenant tradition par excellence.[13] "Covenant" is not to be understood as simply a religious slogan, nor as one model among many for Israel's faith. It is rather the quintessential, normative theological-ethical accent of Israel's faith. Deuteronomy offers covenant as a radical and systematic alternative to the politics of autonomy, the economics of exploitation, and the theology of self-indulgence. The model of social reality offered in Deuteronomy is that this community—in all its socioeconomic, political, and military aspects—is relational, with members taking responsibility for their neighbors. This notion of social reality touches every phase of social interaction and every exercise of social power. The pervasive disciplines to which Deuteronomy summons Israel is precisely to give up autonomy for the sake of committed, neighborly relatedness.

I may cite three facets of this summons:

Economically, the practice of neighborliness is in "the year of release" (Deut. 15:1-18). This command, likely the quintessence of neighborliness, seeks to prevent the emergence of a permanent underclass by providing that regularly and frequently, the poor shall have their debts canceled and be equipped for reentry into the economy in a viable way.[14] It is impossible to overstate the radicalness and subversive threat of this provision that undermines any conventional economic practice, and that intends to make Israel a peculiar community in the world.

Liturgically, the teaching of Deuteronomy accents the Passover as an affirmation that Israel's life shall be intentionally situated in the memory of the exodus. If, as is generally judged, Deuteronomy is set in an Assyrian context, then this liturgical practice transfers the Egyptian miracle into an Assyrian matrix. In 2 Kings 23:21-23, moreover, in a text intimately linked to Deuteronomy, King Josiah is presented as the one who recovers Passover as a disciplined way of sustaining a peculiar identity in the world.

Politically, Deuteronomy acknowledges royal power and severely curbs its drive for autonomous control. The law envisions Torah-based power, for the king is enjoined to study "this torah" day and night, so that even Davidic kinship is finally located in the covenantal context of Deuteronomy (Deut. 17:14-20). Negatively, moreover, the king is to shun the easy temptations of commoditization by refusing accumulation of silver, gold, wives, horses, or chariots. All of those possible gains are fundamentally irrelevant to a covenantal community, and such offers are simply distortions of Israel's true life.

To be sure, the traditions of Isaiah (royal), Micah (peasant), and Deuteronomy (Mosaic-covenantal) give differing nuance to the life of Judah. All are agreed, however, that in every sphere of its life, Judah must be a community of intentional resistance, refusing to let dominant, imperial definitions confiscate the life of Judah. The community is enjoined to great vigilance, lest it lose its raison d'être, which is as a Yahwistic, alternative mode of life in a world of acquisitive, exploitative power (compare Deut. 8:1-20).

III

Israel is an intentional, distinctive community in a world dominated by Babylon. According to common critical judgment, Israel's situation in Babylon as deported, displaced exiles is the clearest, least complicated moment of *intentional community* vis-à-vis *dominating power* (compare Ps. 137 for a voicing of the mood of the exiles).[15] Because the exiles are now displaced from their homeland and from all its sustaining institutional markers, the power of Babylonian culture to assimilate and the capacity of the Babylonian economy to substitute satiation for a faith identity are indeed an intense threat. The intensity of the threat in turn evokes the most intentional efforts at community maintenance. Of the many efforts at such maintenance, I will mention two.

First, it is conventional to locate the Priestly material of Genesis-Numbers in the exile, as a strategy for sustaining the *sacramental* sense of community.[16] The Priestly materials, which became the decisive ordering of Israel's Torah, are aimed toward the maintenance of *order* in a social context of acute disorder and chaos. The Jews in exile had no stable reference points (as with appeal to the temple), and so this tradition offers alternative practices in lieu of such supports. In Genesis 1:1—2:4a, the tradition provides a litany that is presumably liturgical, whereby the creation is celebrated, affirmed, and experienced as an ordered, reliable environment for life. That is, the liturgy itself intends to challenge and override the chaos of exilic social circumstance. Among the features that provide liturgical stability are the following:

• The assurance that God's powerful spirit is at work in the world, which is therefore an arena of blessing. Generativity of life is assured there.

• The process of ordering is articulated in *separating* elements of creation into their proper zones (Gen. 1:4, 6, 7, 14) and by assuring that all fruitfulness is "of every kind" (Gen. 1:21, 24-25). This is a world in which nothing is out of place.

• The ordering is repeatedly acknowledged to be "good," and finally "very good." It is probable that "good" here means lovely, aesthetically pleasing. This is a beautiful place in which to reside!

• The liturgy culminates in sabbath rest, whereby the members of this community desist from production, and do so without anxiety. They are sure that the world will hold, because it is authorized by the creator God.

We may imagine that this liturgy provided focus, coherence, and assurance that made the exiles less vulnerable to the threats and to the seductions of Babylon. This tradition, however, championed not only order, but also *presence*.[17] Thus the Priestly materials also provide the exactitude of authorizing (Exodus 25–31) and construction (Exodus 35–40) of a tabernacle as a place suitable for God's dwelling in the midst of Israel. With great care and attentiveness, according to this imaginative tradition, Israel is able to host the holiness of God, thereby acknowledging that even severe cultural dislocation cannot impede Israel's ready access to the God it loves and serves.

In addition to *order and presence,* this tradition also insists on a *self-conscious ethic* commensurate with God's own holiness:

You shall be holy, for I the LORD your God am holy. (Lev. 19:2)

The commands of Leviticus, which often strike us as excessively punctilious, are an effort to assure the community of a distinctiveness that devotes its entire existence to the will and purpose of Yahweh. This tradition quite clearly accepts a vocation of oddity:

You shall not do as they do in the land of Egypt, where you have lived, and you shall not do as they do in the land of Canaan, to which I am bringing you. (Lev. 18:3)

This text does not mention Babylon, for such a mention here would be anachronistic. If, however, the text is dated to the sixth century, then we may understand "Egypt" and "Canaan" as capable of extrapolation to Babylon. Moreover,

I have separated you from the peoples. You shall therefore make a distinction between the clean animals and the unclean . . . . (Lev. 20:24-25)

The practice of distinctiveness must pervade every aspect and dimension of Israel's life, down to the last small detail.

Second, this sacramental practice of distinctiveness in the Priestly tradition has as its counterpoint a much more dynamic, promissory tradition in the poetry of Isa. 40–55. Whereas the Priestly material makes the case for distinctiveness in a rather static way, the Isaiah poetry calls Israel to enact a transformed life in the world. Thus the gospel announcement of Yahweh's new governance surges in upon Israel, creating a new social possibility for homecoming and a new ground for communal joy:

> O Jerusalem, herald of good tidings,
>   lift it up, do not fear;
> say to the cities of Judah,
>   "Here is your God." (Isa. 40:9)

> How beautiful upon the mountains
>   are the feet of the messenger . . .
> who says to Zion, "Your God reigns." (Isa. 52:7)

In these twin assertions, the power of Babylon is said to be broken. Babylonian gods are defeated. Babylonian power is overcome. Babylonian futures are nullified. Babylonian definitions of reality are overthrown.

Israel is free for life under the aegis of Yahweh, who wills well-being, justice, and homecoming. This poet is a voice of hope to a community near despair, ready to give up on Yahweh. Indeed, great oppressive regimes aim at despair, for the killing of a hope-filled future renders displaced people powerless and easy to administer. Thus the poetic, lyrical, liturgical practice of hope is foundational for the sustenance of an odd community. Such practices of course can easily become sloganeering self-deception, unless the community is able to point to signs in the actual course of affairs. Poetic imagination in Isaiah was able to transpose observed public events into gifts Yahweh had performed for Israel. The emancipation of hopefulness engendered liturgical freedom that in turn produced ethical, and eventually, geographical freedom. This community knows itself, sooner or later, to be headed home in a triumphant procession (compare Isa. 35:8-10; 40:3-5).

The text makers in exile were able to defeat the grip that Babylonian hegemony had upon the imagination of Israel. The *sacramental* and the *lyrical* both operate in the same tension; it is equally clear that both articulations and practices were crucial for the survival and missional buoyancy of this community so deeply in jeopardy.

IV

Israel is an intentional, distinctive community in a world dominated by Persia. The rise of Persia under the leadership of Cyrus had been voiced and anticipated in Isa. 44:28—45:7 as a gift from Yahweh for the sake of the community of exiles. And indeed, it is evident that compared to Babylon's policy of coerced deportation, Persian policy toward conquered peoples (including the Jews) was much more humane, permitting deported peoples to go home and providing financial assistance for local religion. For that reason the interaction between Persian power and Jewish distinctiveness is not at all antagonistic, for the key agents of Jewish distinctiveness, Ezra and Nehemiah, are authorized and funded by Persia.

It is not for nothing that the peculiar work of Ezra and Nehemiah is commonly termed a "reform." Their work is the imposition of a particularly intense form of Judaism, propelled by a self-assured, self-conscious elite company of Babylonian Jews, upon the populace of Jerusalem. These leaders are indeed fanatical about the reestablishment of a self-conscious, intentional community of discipline that will not accommodate or compromise with cultural pressures.[18] To be sure, these reform measures have often been viewed, especially according to Christian stereotype, as narrow and legalistic. They must, however, be understood in a context in which it seemed clear that the very future and survival of Judaism required stringent and demanding measures.

Concerning the enactment of distinctiveness that characterizes the work of Ezra and Nehemiah, I will mention four elements:

• In what is regarded as the founding event of postexilic Judaism, Ezra convenes "all who could hear with understanding" to the promulgation of the Torah, whereby Judaism is marked as a community that listens to the lore and commands of Yahweh's Torah and shapes its life in glad response to it (Neh. 8:1-12). This peculiar community is not self-generated, but understands itself in terms of a special authorization in a script available for steady and regular, attentive reiteration.

• The word event of Torah is matched by the sacramental gesture of the Festival of Booths, whereby Israel bodily reenacts the ancient memories of the wilderness sojourn (Neh. 8:13-18). In this act, Israel is made freshly aware of the precarious character of its life and the generosity of God as the ground of its survival and well-being.

• The reformers introduce and require rigorous disciplines commensurate with the jeopardy of evaporation. These include separation from non-Jews (Neh. 13:1-3); rejection of mixed marriages (13:27-31); which moves in the direction of "ethnic cleansing"; and the observation and payment of regular offerings (10:32-39). While these provisions may strike us as excessive, it is evident that they aim at bringing every aspect of communal life under the intentional governance of Yahweh. Nothing falls outside that commitment.

• Most remarkably, Nehemiah insists on a communitarian economics by rejecting the charging of interest within the community and by binding the haves and have-nots into a practical and effective economic covenant (5:1-13).

It is this series of reforms that sets later Judaism on its way as a community of discipline and obedience. At the end of the Persian period and the rise of Hellenism under Alexander, the maintenance of distinctive

Jewishness became urgent. This does not mean that this community remained isolated or insulated. It is clear, and surely inevitable, that Judaism, in a Hellenistic environment, engaged intensely with culture, thus producing what we have come to call "Hellenistic Judaism."[19] What strikes us, however, is not the extent of accommodation, but the capacity to maintain, in an identifiable, self-conscious way, a Jewish sense of life in the world.

V

This long review has provided us a long-term menu for Israel's sense of self through the vagaries and challenges of historical experience. We may, from this review, draw three conclusions:

1. In all of these periods, Israel's work of resistance and durability features some common elements:

• Israel as a self-conscious community of faith is in every phase of this history profoundly in jeopardy in relation to its context. Its survival depends upon a fluid capacity for resistance and embrace that is in large part pragmatic. But that pragmatic quality can never eliminate the risk.

• There are socioeconomic, political factors and ethnic sensibilities at work in this process in every season. At its core, however, the oddness of this community is theological; it is rooted in the reality of Yahweh, who is seen to be demanding and legitimating.

• Such a community requires intentional and rigorous disciplines, so intentional and rigorous that outsiders may view them as excessively demanding. But such discipline is a life-and-death matter. Israel under threat is never an easy "therapeutic" community, and faith in Yahweh is not a massage. It is the embrace and practice of a destiny that makes costly demands in the name of Yahweh.

• At the center of these demands are indeed *word and sacrament*—word understood as text production, text reiteration, and text interpretation; sacrament as bodily acts that dramatize full commitment to the rigors.

2. The visible, intentional community of faith that is our present concern is not preoccupied with any of these empires. While we may each one give a different name to our comparable matrix of faith identity, I suggest that the task of the beloved community now is *vis-à-vis the "money economy" of Western postindustrial technology that sweeps all before it,* and that seemingly cannot be resisted.[20] The reality of this enterprise—rooted in commodity, aimed at satiation, and unhesitant about brutality—poses acute questions and challenges for a distinctive community of faith. While this imperial context is perhaps not more dangerous than any of these others I have named, it is the one for our time and place.

Perhaps this review may suggest some of the particularities that we may enact as our own, whereby to refuse the complete triumph of military consumerism. Thus the real quarrel is rightly not between believing Christian liberals and believing Christian conservatives, or between publicly inclined and sectarianly inclined Christians; it is rather an issue between baptized Christians and those for whom Yahweh has dropped out of the narrative of the world. Distinctiveness depends upon telling and enacting the story of the world with Yahweh—the governor of Israel and the Lord of the church—as the key character.

3. The new situation of Christianity in the West, with the demise of institutional power, poses problems but also offers great opportunities for a serious church. Because the church has been dominant in the West, often in brutalizing ways, its present circumstance cannot be at all likened to the ongoing social location of Jews. Having said that, it is nonetheless possible that in a new decentered position, *Christians may learn from Jews.* I commend the study of Jacob Neusner concerning *The Enchantments of Israel,* the daily disciplines and practices of Judaism that keep identity vibrant and available.[21] Neusner observes that such practices abet the daily task of "imaging Jewishness," for without such intentional imagination, says Neusner, Jews cannot be sustained in faith.[22]

Mutatis mutandis, the new cultural dislocation and disestablishment of the church suggest a like mandate of imagination for Christians. Daily imagining of Christian-baptismal identity is urgent. Word and sacrament are decisive practices in this task. Finally, however, the urgency is to opt for an actual social reality in which Yahweh is a key player. Powerful forces want to defeat that account of reality. It is the vocation of this peculiar community of faith to keep available and credible the Yahweh account of reality. That requires careful utterance and daring enactment, clear thinking and bold living.

7   Exodus in the Plural (Amos 9:7)

Sᴉɴᴄᴇ ᴛʜᴇ ᴇᴍᴇʀɢᴇɴᴄᴇ ᴏꜰ ᴀ ᴄʀɪᴛɪᴄᴀʟ ᴄᴏɴꜱᴇɴꜱᴜꜱ ɪɴ Oʟᴅ Tᴇꜱᴛᴀᴍᴇɴᴛ study in the nineteenth century, it has been agreed that the prophecy of Amos, preserved as the book of Amos, provides the first clear, uncontested evidence that Israel had arrived at ethical monotheism.[1] Indeed, liberal developmentalism came to regard the words of Amos as the first utterance of "Israel's normative faith." This scholarly consensus concerning "ethical monotheism" was viewed in such interpretation as a great positive victory over (a) polytheism, which was primitive and ignoble, and (b) cultic religion, which smacked of magic and manipulation. That is, classical liberal scholarship, with its unabashed Christian commitments, wedded to a developmental notion of Israel's faith, viewed Amos as the clear emergence of what is right and good and noble, which would eventuate in Christianity. There could be no going back on this monotheism.[2]

I

Nineteenth-century developmentalism did not so readily recognize that ethical monotheism, insofar as that is a correct judgment about Amos, constituted not only a great theological gain in the history of Israelite religion, but also brought with it an enormous ideological temptation, a temptation most often readily accepted. It was proudly and doxologically affirmed that Yahweh was one, or that Yahweh was the only one,[3] and moreover, that this one and only Yahweh had as a partner a one and only people Israel, so that there was taken to be a complete commensurability between the "onlyness" of Yahweh and the "onlyness" of Israel.[4] And where the "onlyness" of Yahweh has as an adjunct affirmation namely the onlyness of Israel, it is self-evident that ideological temptation to absolutize Israel along with an absolute Yahweh is almost irresistible.

We may consider two impetuses for this ideological extension of the "onlyness" of Yahweh to include the "onlyness" of Israel, which I shall term "mono-ideology."[5] The first impetus, not at all surprising, is the Davidic-Solomonic, royal ideology that insisted upon a close connection between Yahweh and royal Israel as a way of giving theological legitimation to political power. Indeed, Rainer Albertz has suggested that monotheism becomes an indispensable counterpart to the claims of monarchy, and that monotheism in Israel emerges only as needed for monarchy.[6]

This ideological combination of one God and one people is evident in David's response to Yahweh's legitimating oracle uttered by Samuel in 2 Sam. 7. In the oracle, Yahweh through Samuel promises to David:

> I will raise up your offspring after you, who shall come forth from
> your body, and I will establish his kingdom. He shall build a house
> for my name, and I will establish the throne of his kingdom forever.
> I will be a father to him, and he shall be a son to me. When he com-
> mits iniquity, I will punish him with a rod such as mortals use, with
> blows inflicted by human beings. But I will not take my steadfast
> love from him, as I took it from Saul, whom I put away from before
> you. Your house and your kingdom shall be made sure forever
> before me; your throne shall be established forever. (vv. 12-16)

Yahweh makes an open-ended, unconditional promise to the dynasty.

In his reception of this oracle (vv. 18-29), David articulates due deference
to Yahweh and his own unworthiness (vv. 18-21). But then David moves
promptly to hold Yahweh to Yahweh's promise (vv. 28-29). In the middle of
this affirmation, David breaks out in doxology concerning the incomparability of Yahweh:

> Therefore you are great, O LORD God; for there is no one like you,
> and there is no God besides you, according to all that we have heard
> with our ears. (v. 22)[7]

This doxological assertion, however, is followed immediately by a parallel
claim for Israel, that is, royal Israel:

> Who is like your people, like Israel? Is there another nation on earth
> whose God went to redeem it as a people, and to make a name for
> himself, doing great and awesome things for them, by driving out
> before his people nations and their gods? And you established your
> people Israel for yourself to be your people forever; and you O
> LORD, became their God. (vv. 23-24)

There is no God like Yahweh. There is no people like Israel. Israel's incomparability is derivative from and shaped by the singular, irreversible,
incomparable commitment of Yahweh to Israel. Thus we arrive not only at
monotheism but also at mono-ethnism, or mono-people. The rhetorical
question of v. 23, "Who is like your people, like Israel? Is there another
nation on earth . . . ?" requires a negative answer. There is none like Israel.
There is not another nation on earth whose God wants to redeem it as a
people. The claim of Yahweh is now deeply and intimately tied to the claim
of Israel. There is not room on this horizon for any other people.

The second impetus for this remarkable mono-linkage is in Deuteronomic theology, likely the source of the exclusive covenantal relation
between Yahweh and Israel, and surely the proximate source of the "Yahweh alone" party in Israel.[8] The ideological intention of the Deuteronomic tradition is not so simple and straightforward as is the royal ideology we

have just cited, for it is at the same time rooted in the Mosaic covenant and yet makes room for royal claims.[9] It is plausible that in the figure of Josiah, the model king of the Deuteronomists, we see the Deuteronomic hope for a Davidic king fully committed to the Mosaic Torah (compare Deut. 17:14-20), thus faithfully honoring both traditions.[10]

However that may be concerning the Deuteronomic theology, there is no doubt that the traditions of Deuteronomy also attach singular claims for Israel to the singular claims made for Yahweh. This is evident in the "centralizing" tendency of Deuteronomy, concerning the cult place in Jerusalem. Just as there is only one Yahweh, so there is only one right place of worship:

> But you shall seek the place that the LORD your God will choose out of all your tribes as his habitation to put his name there. You shall go there, bringing there your burnt offerings and your sacrifices, your tithes and your donations, your votive gifts, your freewill offerings, and the firstlings of your herds and flocks. And you shall eat there in the presence of the LORD your God, you and your household together, rejoicing in all the undertakings in which the LORD your God has blessed you. . . . But only at the place that the LORD will choose in one of your tribes—there you shall offer your burnt offerings and there you shall do everything I command you. (Deut. 12:5-7, 14)

It is of course correct that the tradition of Deuteronomy tries to distance itself from the crass claims of presence made by high royal theology, by the device of "the name."[11] Thus it is not Yahweh, but Yahweh's "name," that is in Jerusalem. Given that provision, however, it is unambiguous that the Deuteronomic traditions were powerful in generating the view that the *one Yahweh* must be worshiped only in the *one place* by the *one people* of Yahweh. And while the program of Deuteronomy may have been in the interest of purging theological deviations in the service of the purity of Yahwism, there is also no doubt that mono-place theology had an ideological dimension in legitimating the royal-scribal-Levitical interpretive claims of Jerusalem.

In a somewhat later text from the same tradition, one can see this ideological claim that attaches Israel to Yahweh with considerable force:

> You must observe them diligently, for this will show your wisdom and discernment to the peoples, who, when they hear all these statutes, will say, "Surely this great nation is a wise and discerning people!" For what other great nation has a god so near to it as the LORD our God is whenever we call to him? And what other great nation has statutes and ordinances as just as this entire law that I am setting before you today? (Deut. 4:5-8)

The evident intention of this statement is to make a bid for obedience to the Torah. The subtext of the statement, however, is that *only Israel* has a God so near, and *only Israel* has a Torah so just, that is, *only Israel* can claim to be peculiarly privileged in the world of the nations. Thus what purports to be a theological affirmation of "only Yahweh" turns out to be a claim, in rather blatant ways, for "only Israel."

Now if "Israel" is to be understood simply as a theological entity bound in covenant to Yahweh and extant in history only to obey Torah, this singular and exclusive linkage to Yahweh is not a drastic problem. It yields something like a sound ecclesiology, albeit a triumphalist one. The inescapable problem, of course, is that Israel (and belatedly the church) is never simply a theological entity, but it is always a socioeconomic-political entity, alive to issues of power, and therefore endlessly capable of committing overt ideological claims for itself.

Thus it takes no great imagination to anticipate that, with royal claims that assert the Yahwistic oddity of Israel (as in 2 Sam. 7:11-16) and Deuteronomic claims that assert the Yahwistic oddity of Israel (Deut. 12:5-7, 14; 4:5-8), Israel will be prepared, uncritically, to transpose its theological claim of "ethical monotheism" into an ideological claim for the singularity, peculiarity, and privilege of Israel as a political entity in the world. This ideological claim, I propose, in the eighth century is not only an understandable outcome of emergent monotheism, but it is an outcome that was proposed, propelled, and driven by the needs of monarchy and by that rather ginger support of monarchy, namely, the Deuteronomic school.

Thus while nineteenth-century scholarship, with its developmentalist inclination, would celebrate the emergence of ethical monotheism, ideology criticism at the end of the twentieth century can notice that what is a theological gain in Israel can be recognized, at the same instant, as a problematic and seductive assertion.[12] This assertion enabled Israel to imagine itself as privileged, in every sphere of life, as Yahweh's unrivaled and inalienable partner.

II

The problematic of emerging ethical monotheism in Israel is this: is it possible to make a theological claim for Yahweh that is not shot through with ideological accoutrements for Israel? We are wont to answer, "Yes, it is possible." The evidence in the Old Testament is not that it is impossible, but that it is exceedingly improbable. In any case, on the ground, monotheism is problematic as a social practice, because it invites all kinds of reductionisms that are taken to be equated with or commensurate with, or in any case inevitably derived from, Yahweh's singleness.

It is into such a situation that the prophet Amos apparently uttered his word.[13] The problem he addressed was not that the Israelites did not believe in Yahweh, but that they believed too much. They believed not only that Yahweh alone is God, but that Israel alone is Yahweh's people. A consequence of this ideological linkage was that Israel became self-satisfied in its ethics and in its worship, so that its very "orthodoxy" became a warrant for self-indulgence (compare Amos 4:4-5; 6:1-6).[14]

In countering this distortion of Yahwism (that passed for orthodoxy in context), the strategy of Amos is to accept the high claims of Yahwism and then to turn those claims against Israel.[15] Thus in the Oracles against the Nations (1:3—2:16), Amos speaks Yahweh's harsh judgment against the nations, only to circle Israel's geographical environment and then to deliver the harshest judgment against Judah (2:4-5) and Israel (2:6-26).[16] In the succinct statement of Amos 3:2, the poet, in the first two lines, accepts Israel's exclusive claim upon Yahweh, apparently alluding back to the ancestral traditions of Genesis (12:3; 18:19). Indeed, the introduction of 3:1 appeals precisely to the exodus, the primal "electing" deed of Yahweh. But those appeals to the tradition are utilized by the poet as a rhetorical setup for the harsh judgment of the second half of the verse:

> Therefore I will punish you
> for all your iniquities. (3:2b)

The "therefore" (*'al-ken*) of this phrase suggests that the very tradition of chosenness (here "known") is the ground and the reason for severe judgment. Thus Amos must struggle with an ethical, monotheistic Yahwism that has been drawn too tightly into self-confidence, and that has issued in a distorting self-sufficiency.

In this chapter, I propose to deal with only one verse, which presents the poet as struggling precisely against the settled orthodoxy that is problematic. The poetic lines of 9:7 seem to stand alone, without a connection to what precedes or follows them:

> Are you not like the Ethiopians to me,
> O people of Israel? says the LORD.
> Did I not bring Israel up from the land of Egypt,
> and the Philistines from Caphtor and the Arameans
> from Kir?

Francis I. Anderson and David Noel Freedman treat the verse in connection with v. 8, so that v. 7 functions for v. 8 by giving the warrant for the judgment, in the same way that the two parts of 3:2 relate to each other.[17] That connection may be correct, but it is not required by the text, and in any case falls beyond the scope of my concern here. It is my suggestion that Amos seeks to undermine the assured mono-ideology of Israel—mono-Yahweh, mono-Israel, perhaps mono-Jerusalem[18]—by introducing a radical pluralism into the character of Yahwism, a pluralism that subverts Israel's self-confident mono-faith.

The three-line utterance of 9:7 is organized into two rhetorical questions, broken only by the authorizing formula, "says the LORD." The first question ends in a vocative, "people of Israel,"[19] so that this is a direct and intimate appeal, acknowledging Yahweh's attentiveness to Israel. It is to those who are fully self-conscious about their identity as the Israel of God that this question is addressed. The question posed is about the likeness, comparability, and similarity of Israel and the Ethiopians (Cushites). The formulation in Hebrew is even more shocking than our usual reading, because "Ethiopians" precedes "you": "Are not the Ethiopians like you?"

The question is not clear about its expected answer. At our distance, we are prepared to assume that the answer is "yes." "Yes," the Ethiopians are like us. But the entire ideological development of Israel, royal and Deuteronomic, had prepared the answer "no." "No," the Ethiopians are not like us. "No," no one is like us.[20] The question is made more demanding by the indirect object, "to me," that is, to Yahweh. Now the comparison of Israel and Cush is not territorial or political or ethnic or linguistic. It is Yahwistic: alike to Yahweh.

Israel of course does not answer. The poet does not seem to have waited for an answer. It might have been wise for Israel to anticipate the ploy of Ezekiel who, when asked an equally demanding question, answered, "O Lord GOD, you know" (Ezek. 37:3). But of course Israel, in the face of Amos, could not beg off as did the later prophet, because Israel did know the answer in its self-congratulatory mono-faith; Israel was clear that there is no other such God, no other such people, with a God so near and a Torah so righteous. Clearly the putting of the question throws all such uncritical confidence into confusion.[21] The "to me" of the question means that Yahweh stands outside the cozy reductions of certitude and confidence that marked Israel's theopolitics.

The second question of our text, introduced by the same interrogative particle with a negative, is more complex. It falls into two parts, except that the two parts cannot be separated. The first part is easy enough:

> Did I not bring Israel up from the land of Egypt?

Of course! Amos has already affirmed that (2:10; 3:1).[22] Israel has affirmed that claim since Moses. The problem of course is that the question does not end there. If it did, it could be easily answered. It continues uninterrupted, with a simple conjunction—"and"—without a new or even reiterated verb. The same verb, "bring up," still functions and governs the second half of the question. Only now the object of this good and familiar verb, the exodus verb, consists in two (bad!) peoples, never before linked to Israel's exodus verb or to Israel's theological discourse. The question permits an oxymoron:

> bring up . . . Philistines,
> bring up . . . Arameans.

The lines use a perfectly good salvific verb ("bring up") with Yahweh as subject, related to enemies. (Notice that the modern state of Israel is also involved in conflicts in the Gaza Strip and the Golan Heights. In geopolitical terms, nothing has changed.)

The listeners to Amos surely wanted to answer the first line of the second question with a resounding "yes," and the second with a militant "no." The problem for such an inclination is that it is only one question, and it admits of only one answer. To answer "no" is to give up, in the first line, the identity-giving claim of tradition. To answer "yes" is to give up the mono-claim of Yahwistic "ethical monotheism," as understood in royal and Deuteronomic traditions. So Israel (wisely?; compare Amos 5:13) does not answer. Israel does not answer "no," because it will not give up its positive claim upon the God of Exodus. It will not answer "yes," because that answer would destroy the ideological "mono" and open Yahweh up to a plurality of exoduses beyond Israel, which Israel cannot countenance. John Barton comments upon the harshness of this option: "When everybody is somebody, then no one's anybody."[23] Israel had become somebody by its singular, exclusivist claim, which in three quick lines is placed into deep jeopardy.

III

But of course, the question is answered "yes." It is answered "yes" by the literary force of the entire Amos tradition. It is answered "yes," moreover, by Yahweh, the asker of the question, who will not be contained in or domesticated by Israel's exclusivist ideology. It is possible, as developmentalists have done, to take this as a statement of Yahweh's monotheism, that is, Yahweh governs all nations as Yahweh's scope of governance expands. I wish, however, to move in a counterdirection: that the text wished to expose and subvert Israel's mono-faith into a radical pluralism that resists every ideological containment.

Consider first what happens to Yahweh in this odd and threatening utterance. Yahweh attests, here in Yahweh's own words, to have many client peoples to whom Yahweh attends in powerful, intervening ways, client peoples who are Israel's long-standing enemies. There is, according to this, no single "salvation history," no fixed line of "God's mighty deeds," for such "mighty deeds" happen in many places, many of which are beyond the purview of Israel's orthodoxy. That much seems unarguable, if Yahweh's double question requires a twofold "yes," as seems evident in the rhetoric.

Let me, however, venture beyond that conclusion about Yahweh that is inescapable in order to extrapolate more from what we know of the exodus. The exodus event, as given us in the liberation liturgy of Exod. 1–15, concerns a community of Israelite-Hebrew slaves who, so far as we know, know nothing of Genesis.[24] All we are told of them, in the narrative itself, is that they were in slavery of an oppressive kind, for the Bible prefers to operate narratively *in media res,* in the midst of things.

The account in Exodus concerns *"a new king"* who oppressed (Exod. 1:8); *midwives* who "feared God" (notice, not Yahweh) and so outwitted Pharaoh (1:17); and the birth of *baby Moses* (2:1-10), who promptly becomes a terrorist and a fugitive (12:11-22). The narrative oddly proceeds this far without reference to Yahweh.

The concluding preliminary comment in 2:23-25 concerns the death of the harsh king and the reactive effect upon Israel who "groaned and cried out."[25] What strikes me about this narrative is that without any theological self-awareness and without any explicit reference to Yahweh, the exodus narrative is set in motion by slaves who seize a moment of social upheaval (the death of the king) and cry out. They bring their pain to speech; they do not cry out because they are believers, but only because they hurt. They do not cry out because they know the book of Genesis and the promises of God, but because they face the irreducible human datum of unbearable suffering. That is all. The rest is the response of Yahweh who "heard, remembered, looked, and took notice" (2:25). Israel voiced its unbearable situation, to which Yahweh is drawn like an insect to the light. And thus Exodus.

Now between this full, well-known account of Israel's liberation and the sparse reference to the Philistines and Arameans in the utterance of Amos, there is not much that is comparable. One is situated in a complete narrative; the other receives only a terse mention. More than that we must imagine. The prophet Amos, by his ideology-shattering rhetorical questions, invites us to imagine that these two traditional enemies of Israel, the Philistines and the Arameans, have a history with Yahweh not unlike Israel's history with Yahweh, even though that history is not known to Israel. We may of course wonder how Amos knows and alludes to such a history to which Israel has no access. The answer to that question is that Amos's vigorous capacity to imagine the pluralistic propensity of Yahweh permits him to know and imagine facets of lived reality from which Israel is blocked by its mono-ideology.

Thus here I imagine that the "hidden history" of the Philistines and the Arameans is, *mutatis mutandis,* closely parallel to the liberated history of Israel.[26]

• Like Israel, the Philistines and the Arameans found themselves in an oppressive situation, though the references to Caphtor and Kir tell us little that we can understand about their past. From Israel's life with Yahweh, it is evident that all peoples live in such a zone of abusiveness, sometimes as victims, sometimes as perpetrators.

• Like Israel, the Philistines and the Arameans were hopelessly embedded in a situation of oppressiveness, where for a long period they could only endure in silence the demanding power of the overlord. Many peoples are like Israel in this season of powerlessness, powerless until a moment of rupture.

• Like Israel, the Philistines and the Arameans were deeply in touch with their history-denying pain, and they watched for a moment when the silence could be broken. When the time came, we may imagine, they groaned and cried out, as the oppressed are wont to do, when the cry and the groan are thought to be worth the risk.

• Like Israel the cry of the Philistines and the Arameans "rose up to God." Note well, they did not cry out to Yahweh, for they were not Yahwists. Indeed, like Israel, they did not even cry out "to God." But as the cry of Israel "rose up to God," so we may imagine the cry of these restive neighbors "rose up to God," for this God is oddly and characteristically attentive to the cry of the bondaged who find enough voice to risk self-announcement, that is, who become agents of their own history.[27]

• The rest, as they say, "is history." Israel understood that God "heard, saw, knew, remembered, and came down to save," out of which came a new people in history. In parallel fashion, so Amos proposes, Yahweh did the same for these other peoples, who emerged in history, liberated by the work of Yahweh, the God of Israel and the God of many oppressed client peoples.

Of course, we have no data for this scenario of matters. I suggest only that Amos's succinct utterance requires some such scenario. It may be that we are permitted to generalize, to say that the Philistines and the Arameans are representative communities, so that all of human history is offered by Amos as a scenario of Yahwistic liberation. Or, if we refuse such generalization, we may only say that Amos offers two such parallels to Israel, or three if we include the Ethiopians in the second question. Either way, the story line of the exodus has substance outside the scope of Israel's life and liturgy.

IV

Now it is clear that Amos's utterance has no special concern for the Philistines or the Arameans (compare 1:3-5), except to assert that they also are under the governance of Yahweh's sovereign intentionality. It is beyond doubt that the utterance of Amos intends to have its primary effect upon Israel, to jar Israel's mono-ideology and to defeat Israel's sense of exceptionalism.

When Amos finishes this double question, Israel is left without its illusion that it monopolizes Yahweh. Israel is disabused of its self-congratulatory indifference and self-confidence, which issue in a cult of satiation and an ethic of aggrandizement. Amos does not deny Israel's self-identity as a people of the exodus. He denies only the monopolistic claim made as the only exodus subject of the only exodus event by the only exodus God.

Beyond this remarkable assault upon Israel's claim to preference and privilege, which surely is the intent of the utterance, we may suggest that something happens to Yahweh as well in the process of this utterance, as an inescapable by-product of shattering Israel's mono-ideology. There is no doubt that the main claim of that mono-ideology pertains not only to Israel, but also to Yahweh, so that the claim of exclusive commitment may apply in both directions. That is, it is not only affirmed in the stylized utterance of Yahweh,

> I shall be your God, i.e., no other God,

but it is also affirmed,

> You shall be my people, i.e., the only people of Yahweh.[28]

Given the "hidden histories" of the Philistines and the Arameans, however, we are given a glimpse of Yahweh's hidden history, that is, Yahweh's long-term interaction with other peoples about which Israel knows nothing and wants to know nothing.

Yahweh, it turns out in this utterance, has other partners who are subjects of Yahweh's propensity to liberation. Presumably these other peoples "groaned and cried out" in their own language, to which Yahweh responded. We may, moreover, wonder if perhaps these other peoples had behind their exoduses a promissory Genesis, and if perhaps the exodus of these other peoples issued in a form of covenant, commandment, and obedience. We are told none of that. And we are lacking in any such evidence. But Amos does clearly require his listeners to entertain the subversive notion that Yahweh is at work in other ways, in other histories, in order to effect other liberations. There is to Yahweh, in this imaginative reading, an identifiable core of coherence.[29] Yahweh's self-presentation is everywhere as an exodus God. That is who Yahweh is and that is what Yahweh does. "History" is a series of exodus narratives of which Israel's is one, but not the only one.

Beyond that powerful mark of coherence as a subject, everything else about Yahweh, in this brief utterance, may take many forms, so that Yahweh may be a character in Philistine history or in Syrian history, surely a treasonable shock to those in the mono-ideology that Amos subverts. Moreover, this action of Yahweh, from what we have in this utterance, did not convert these peoples to Yahwism, did not require them to speak Hebrew, and did not submerge their histories as subsets of Israel's history. The liberation wrought by Yahweh left each of these peoples, so much as we know, free to live out and develop their own sense of cultural identity and of freedom. Thus it is fair to imagine that Yahweh, as the exodus God who generated the Philistines, came to be known, if at all, in Philistine modes. And Yahweh as the exodus God who evoked the Syrians to freedom came to be known, if at all, in Syrian modes. Beyond the coherent, pervading mark of exodus intentionality, we may as a consequence imagine that Yahweh is enormously pliable and supple as a participant in the histories of many peoples, not all of which are exact replicas of Israel's narrative or sub-sets of Israel's self-discernment.

V

To be sure, this is only one brief text in a prophetic collection that does in many places assume Israel's exceptionalism, so that too much must not be made of this one verse. Moreover, Amos is only one brief collection in Israel's text that became canonized, and there is no doubt that Amos was situated in the midst of the powerful mono-ideology of the Deuterono-mists.[30] Thus I do not want to overstate the case.

This single verse in the context of the Amos collection and in the larger context of Israel's seductive mono-ideology is evidence that pluralism is voiced in ancient Israel as a critique of reductive mono-ideology. Amos resituates Israel, Yahweh, and the nations by asserting that what is true concerning Yahweh cannot be contained or domesticated into Israel's favorite slogans, categories, or claims. The actual concrete "happened-ness" of Yahweh in the world is much more comprehensive than that, even if it is mostly kept hidden.

It is now conventional, both in the U.S. church and in current cultural con-fusions of U.S. society, to value with nostalgia the good days of "coherence," when the church "willed one thing" and when all of society was ordered around stable, broadly accepted coherences.[31] Conversely, given such a view, which is immune to the thought that such coherence was constituted by an imposition of hegemony, it is held that more recent pluralism is a terrible demise and collapse of all that is good. "Recovery," moreover, will mean an overcoming of pluralism and the reassertion of an ordered hegemony.

There may be some truth in that claim—even though it is not going to happen. But truth or no, I propose that this little two-liner from Amos must stick in the throat of our nostalgic sense of loss and yearning, as it must have stuck in the throat of the mono-ideologues in Israel.

If we take this succinct utterance seriously, the pluriform nature of Yah-weh is a truth that is not negative. It is rather a truth that can emancipate Israel from its deluding mono-ideology, in which what had been a Yahwis-tically enacted gift of truth (the actual exodus) had become a possession and property legitimating imagined self-importance and autonomy. Thus pluriform Yahwism may be seen as a healthy resituation of Israel's life in the world that affirms that there are facets of Yahweh's life not subject to Israel's definition and facets of the life of the world that are not to be placed under Israel's mono-ideological umbrella. There is a deep, dense otherness to Yahweh in human history, which stands as an invitation and principle of criticism, when Israel's faith becomes self-serving ideology. Amos clearly has no fear of pluriform Yahwism, but sees it as a stance from which Israel may revise itself more faithfully and more realistically.

VI

From this reflection upon this single verse in Amos, I wish to draw three concluding reflections:

1. There is, in this subversion of the mono-ideology of ancient Israel, an important critique and warning against a notion of "God's elect people," as it pertains both to Jews and Christians. It is clear that Amos was addressing neither Judaism nor Christianity, but the antecedent of both. And because the ancient Israel addressed by Amos is the antecedent of both derivative communities of faith, the subversive warning applies no more to Judaism than it does to Christianity.

As concerns Judaism, in my judgment, one may draw a warning and critique from Amos concerning the "mystery of Israel," where it is drawn too tightly toward an ethnic Jewishness. I do not cite this verse, in the horizon of Judaism, in order to suggest anything like Christian supersessionism, but only to assert, even in the face of Judaism's unrivaled formal claim as the people of Yahweh, that the density and majesty of Yahweh cannot be contained in any ideological Judaism that weds Yahweh to an ethnic community.

While this warning to and critique of Judaism are not my concern here (nor my proper business as a Christian), the visionary utterance of Amos can be related to two recent Jewish statements concerning Judaism. First, Jon D. Levenson, apropos liberation theology, resists any notion of God's "preferential option" for the marginated that removes the essential Jewishness of God's preference.[32] In the end, however, even Levenson, in his insistence upon Jewish focus, acknowledges that the exodus narrative may be paradigmatic for other communities awaiting God's emancipation.[33] This seems to me congruent with the utterance of Amos.

Second, Jacob Neusner, in a recent argument, has insisted that the definitional mark of Judaism as God's people is simply, singularly, and only adherence to the Torah.[34] Neusner is alert to Christian misconstruals of Judaism as ethnic Jewishness, but is much more concerned with the misconstruals of Judaism among Jews who confuse a community embedded in the mystery of Torah with other, ethnic or cultural markings of Jewishness. In a way even more direct than the comment of Levenson, Neusner seems to me precisely aimed at the concern of Amos, even though, to be sure, Amos focuses upon the exodus and not the Torah.

2. In a volume concerned with Christianity and pluralism and perhaps more precisely Calvinism and pluralism, our interest here has to do with the

Christian spin-offs from the utterance of Amos. As Deuteronomy is a main force for mono-ideology in ancient Judaism, so it is possible to conclude that Calvinism has been a primary force for mono-ideology in modern Christian history, because of its insistence upon God's sovereignty, which is very often allied with socioeconomic-political hegemony.

Given that propensity of Western Christendom in general and Calvinism in particular, if pluralism is not perceived as a threat (as it is in many quarters), it is at least a demanding challenge that a characteristic tilt toward mono-ideology be radically reconsidered. As pluralism in a variety of forms flourishes among us, there is a sharp tendency to want to take refuge in an "old coherence" against pluralism, an old coherence that is variously seen to be theological orthodoxy, but that seems always to be accompanied by a certain kind of sociopolitical hegemony.

Here my concern is not the relation of Christianity to other "Great Religions," but it is the internal life of Christianity. The utterance of Amos has voiced in a forceful way that Yahweh (the God we confess to be fully known in Jesus Christ) is not unilaterally attached to our preferred formulas, practices, or self-identity. There is a profound otherness in Yahweh that is incommensurate with the church, as with Israel. It is my hunch that ours is a time in the church when retrenching into mono-ideology is a severe temptation, but a recognition of the history of Yahweh's otherness, which is fearful and problematic, may be an embrace of prophetic faith. If such a quality in Yahweh's life be embraced, it may be that our preferred theological formulations, liturgic inclinations, and cultural assumptions may be incongruous with the oddness of Yahweh, whose liberating intentions may be allied with and attached to many forms of human life other than our own. The mono-propensities that sound most orthodox may be desperate attempts to reduce Yahweh to safer proportions. Of course, I do not know how far this pluriform reality should be extrapolated to our circumstance. One such extreme extrapolation is the conclusion of Maurice Wiles, in his comment on the reality of divine forgiveness and divine presence apprehended in the cross and in the church:

> Calvary and the institutional church are not necessarily their only instantiations in history.[35]

3. I am sure there is a need for "monoizing" that arises from time to time in the church. But it is not a given that monoizing is in every circumstance the proper work of the church. There are also occasions when monoizing is an act of disobedience, when in God's time pluralizing is required. If both practices on occasion are congruent with God's will and purpose, then we may now (and in any time) have a conversation about which is our appropriate posture, without monoizers assuming that they automatically hold the high ground, high ground that seems almost always to be congruent with vested interest.[36]

What better way, in a paper offered to Shirley Guthrie, than to conclude with a quote from Karl Barth. In thinking, early on, about the relationship between Christian faith and culture, Barth fully affirms that the position of right faith is genuinely open and dialectical. In commenting upon the relation of Christianity to society, and the need to be flexible to the right and to the left, Barth writes:

> Without being disturbed by the inconsistent appearance of it we shall then enjoy the freedom of saying now Yes and now No, and of saying both not as a result of outward change or inward caprice but because we are so moved by the will of God, which has been abundantly proved "good, and acceptable, and perfect." (Rom. 12:2)[37]

Of course, much of "Barthianism" has taken a moment of Barth and hardened it into a principle. But not so Barth.

In commenting upon the work of Barth, Gogarten, and others in this regard, Klaus Scholder comments:

> It is to this freedom to which the Word of God is a summons that Karl Barth was referring at the end of his Tambach lecture . . . There is no need to say anything in support of the justification and the significance of this approach; they are evident. But the question now is whether in the struggle against binding the Word of God to any ideologies a new ideology did not to some extent creep in through the back door, namely the ideology of crisis . . . the absolute No replaces the absolute Yes.[38]

Scholder is explicit in exempting Barth from the tendency to make "No" a new ideology, which he associates especially with Gogarten.

In this regard, the refusal of an *ideology of No* as much as an *ideology of Yes,* which I here transpose into *mono-ideology* and an *ideology of pluralism,* Barth echoes the radical view of Amos. Neither is always and everywhere an act of obedience.

At the end of the Old Testament, prophetic faith knows that Yahwism runs well beyond Israel. Indeed, Yahweh, in the end, has more than one chosen people:

> On that day Israel will be the third with Egypt and Assyria, a blessing in the midst of the earth, whom the LORD of hosts has blessed, saying, "Blessed be Egypt my people, and Assyria the work of my hands, and Israel my heritage." (Isa. 19:24-25)

In our struggle with the matters that preoccupied Amos, it is important to ease our desperate need for control enough to be dazzled at the Holy One of Israel, a dazzling that outruns our need or capacity for our particular mode of coherence. It is more important, as James M. Robinson has observed, that Israel should be endlessly amazed and grateful for its own existence:

For the wonder of Israel, rather than not being at all, is the basic experience of Israel in all its history. The reference to the living God . . . "answers" the question precisely by pointing to the God before whom this wonder at being is constant and inescapable.[39]

The rest may be left to God.

Abbreviations

AB	Anchor Bible
BWANT	Beiträge zur Wissenschaft vom Alten und Neuen Testament
BZAW	Beihefte zur *ZAW*
CBQ	*Catholic Biblical Quarterly*
HSM	Harvard Semitic Monographs
ICC	International Critical Commentary
JBL	*Journal of Biblical Literature*
JSOT	*Journal for the Study of the Old Testament*
JSOTSup	Journal for the Study of the Old Testament— Supplement Series
OBT	Overtures to Biblical Theology
OTL	Old Testament Library
PTMS	Pittsburgh (Princeton) Theological Monograph Series
RB	*Revue biblique*
SBL	Society of Biblical Literature
SBLDS	SBL Dissertation Series
SBT	Studies in Biblical Theology
SVT	Supplements to *VT*
VT	*Vetus Testamentum*
WMANT	Wissenschaftliche Monographien zum Neuen Testament
ZAW	*Zeitschrift für die alttestamentliche Wissenschaft*

Notes

1. Texts That Linger, Words That Explode

This chapter was originally a paper presented at the Society of Biblical Literature (Philadelphia, 1995) in the Frontiers in Biblical Scholarship Lecture Series, jointly sponsored by the Endowment for Biblical Research.

1. Gerhard von Rad, *The Problem of the Hexateuch and Other Essays,* trans. E. W. T. Dicken (New York: McGraw-Hill, 1966) 1–78, and *Old Testament Theology* vol. 1 (San Francisco: Harper and Row, 1962).

2. On the notion of the "Yahweh alone" party, see Morton Smith, *Palestinian Parties and Politics That Shaped the Old Testament* (New York: Columbia University Press, 1971) 110–13 and *passim.* Less directly, see Martin Rose, *Der Ausschlusslichkeitsanspruch Jahwes* (BWANT 6; Berlin: Kohlhammer, 1975).

3. An attempt to counter what I am calling "liberal indifference" seems to me to be a primary concern of Brevard S. Childs. See *Reclaiming the Bible for the Church,* ed. Carl E. Braaten and Robert W. Jenson (Grand Rapids: Eerdmans, 1995). Proponents of this perspective, however, seem completely unaware of the ways in which their approach serves conservative reductionism, and therefore the approach is not, in my judgment, without its own considerable problems.

4. Rachel, in the Genesis narrative, had already died in 35:16-20, well before Jacob's dismay over Joseph's apparent death.

5. See Samuel H. Dresner, *Rachel* (Minneapolis: Fortress Press, 1994).

6. I use the term "son forsaken," because I intend to make an allusion to the nice phrasing of Jürgen Moltmann, *The Crucified God: The Cross of Christ as the Foundation and Criticism of Christian Theology* (London: SCM, 1974), who refers, in the crucifixion of Jesus, to the Son as "father forsaken," and to the Father as "son forsaken." I submit that the figure of Rachel anticipates these claims made in the Christian tradition.

7. Emil Fackenheim, "New Heart and the Old Covenant: On Some Possibilities of a Fraternal Jewish-Christian Reading of the Jewish Bible Today," in *The Divine Helmsman: Studies on God's Control of Human Events,* ed. James L. Crenshaw and Samuel Sandmel (New York: KTAV, 1980) 191–205.

8. Jonathan Kozol, *Rachel and Her Children: Homeless Families in America* (New York: Fawcett Books, 1988).

9. Ernest Nicholson, *Preaching to the Exiles* (Oxford: Blackwell, 1970), saw clearly that the way in which Jehoiachim "cuts" the scroll is an

intentional contrast to the conduct of Josiah in 2 Kings 22:11, who "cuts" his clothes in penitence. See also William L. Holladay, *Jeremiah 2* (Hermeneia; Minneapolis: Fortress Press, 1989) 259–60. On the text of Jeremiah 36, see Walter Brueggemann, "Haunting Book—Haunted People (Jeremiah 36; Luke 4:16-40)," *Word and World* 11 (Winter 1991) 62–68.

10. José Faur, "God as a Writer: Omnipresence and the Art of Dissimulation," *Religion and Intellectual Life* 6 (Spring/Summer 1989) 31–43.

11. George Lindbeck, *The Nature of Doctrine: Religion and Theology in a Postliberal Age* (Philadelphia: Westminster, 1984), develops a grid of three interpretive models, the third being "propositional."

12. Michael Walzer, *Exodus and Revolution* (New York: Basic Books, 1986).

13. On the general theme, see James C. Scott, *Weapons of the Weak* (New Haven: Yale University Press, 1987).

14. On the killing power of silence and the recovery of life through speech, see Rebecca Chopp, *The Power to Speak: Feminism, Language, God* (New York: Crossroad, 1991); Carol Gilligan et al., *Making Connections: The Relational Worlds of Adolescent Girls at Emma Willard School* (Cambridge: Harvard University Press, 1990); Judith L. Herman, *Trauma and Recovery: The Aftermath of Violence: From Domestic Abuse to Political Terror* (New York: Basic Books, 1992); Alice Miller, *Thou Shalt Not Be Aware: Society's Betrayal of the Child*, 2nd ed. (London: Pluto, 1990); and Elaine Scarry, *The Body in Pain: The Making and Unmaking of the World* (New York: Oxford University Press, 1985).

15. On the theme of continuity and discontinuity, see Peter R. Ackroyd, "Continuity: A Contribution to the Study of the Old Testament Religious Tradition," in *Studies in the Religious Tradition of the Old Testament* (London: SCM, 1987) 3–16, and "Continuity and Discontinuity: Rehabilitation and Authentication," also in *Studies in the Religious Tradition*, 31–45.

On the problematic of this theme in relation to Christians and Jews, see the fine essays in *New Directions in Biblical Theology*, ed. Sigfried Pedersen (Leiden: E. J. Brill, 1994).

16. See Walter Brueggemann, "A Shattered Transcendence? Exile and Restoration," in *Biblical Theology: Problems and Perspectives*, ed. Steven J. Kraftchick et al. (Nashville: Abingdon, 1995) 169–82.

17. Gabriel Fackre, "The Place of Israel in Christian Faith," *Gott lieben und seine Gebote halten* [*Loving God and Keeping His Commandments*], ed. Markus Bockmuehl and Helmut Burkhardt (Basel: Brunnen Verlag, 1991) 21–38, has nicely summarized the great variety of positions and postures subsumed under the general rubric of "supersessionism."

18. For a penetrating analysis of the supersessionism in the classical formulations of Christian faith, see Kendall Soulen, *The God of Israel and Christian Theology* (Minneapolis: Fortress Press, 1996).

19. Steven Katz, *The Holocaust in Historical Context* I (Oxford: Oxford

University Press, 1994), and Stephen R. Haynes, *Reluctant Witnesses: Jews and the Christian Imagination* (Louisville: Westminster John Knox, 1995).

20. J. Wayne Baker and Charles S. McCoy, *Fountainhead of Federalism: Heinrich Bullinger and the Covenant Tradition* (Louisville: Westminster John Knox, 1991), have traced the way in which Bullinger, successor to Zwingli in Zurich, became the decisive proponent of "covenant" as a model for theological interpretation and for political practice. More generally, see Stephen Strehle, *Calvinism, Federalism, and Scholasticism: A Study of the Reformed Doctrine of Covenant* (New York: Peter Lang, 1988).

21. Robert N. Bellah, *The Broken Covenant: American Civil Religion in Time of Trial* (Chicago: University of Chicago Press, 1992); James Michener, *The Covenant* (New York: Random House, 1980).

22. See Norbert Lohfink, *The Covenant Never Revoked: Biblical Reflection on Christian-Jewish Dialogue* (New York: Paulist, 1991).

23. On the "everlasting covenant," see Lohfink, *The Covenant Never Revoked,* and Delbert R. Hillers, *Covenant: The History of a Biblical Idea* (Baltimore: Johns Hopkins University Press, 1969).

24. There is a large literature on the genre. See Norman K. Gottwald, *All the Kingdoms of the Earth: Israelite Prophecy and International Relations in the Ancient Near East* (New York: Harper and Row, 1964), and more recently, Paul R. Raabe, "Why Prophetic Oracles against the Nations?" in *Fortunate the Eyes That See: Essays in Honor of David Noel Freedman,* ed. Astrid B. Beck et al. (Grand Rapids: Eerdmans, 1995) 236–57.

25. On the latter text, see Alice O. Bellis, *The Structure and Composition of Jer. 50:2—51:58* (New York: Edwin Mellen, 1994).

26. See Klaus Wengst, "Babylon the Great and the New Jerusalem: The Visionary View of Political Reality in the Revelation of John," in *Politics and Theopolitics in the Bible and Postbiblical Literature,* ed. Henning Graf Reventlow et al. (JSOTSup 171; Sheffield: Sheffield Academic Press, 1994) 189–202. In addition to Rev. 18:7-21, see 14:8, 16:19, and 17:5.

27. Martin Luther, "The Babylonian Captivity of the Church," in *Three Treatises* (Philadelphia: Muhlenburg Press, 1960) 115–260.

28. Philip Wheaton and Duane Shank, *Empire and the Word: Prophetic Parallels Between the Exilic Experience and Central America's Crisis* (Washington: EPICA, 1988).

29. Paul M. Kennedy, *The Rise and Fall of the Great Powers: Economic Change and Military Conflict from 1500 to 2000* (New York: Random House, 1987).

30. There is no doubt that the scribes came to be the critical intellectuals in emerging Judaism. See Joseph Blenkinsopp, *Sage, Priest, Prophet: Religious and Intellectual Leadership in Ancient Israel* (Louisville: Westminster John Knox, 1995) 9–41. Thus it is fair to say,

mutatis mutandis, that the scribes worked at the same issues as belated members of the "biblical guild."

31. John D. Caputo, *Demythologizing Heidegger* (Bloomington: Indiana University Press, 1993).

32. The phrasing of Derrida is from "Force of Law: The Mystical Foundation of Authority" in "Deconstruction and the Possibility of Justice," *Cardoza Law Review* 11 (1990) 919–1045, to which I have not had access. It is quoted by Caputo, *Demythologizing Heidegger,* 193.

33. Ibid., 187.

34. Ibid., 201.

35. Ibid., 201–2.

36. Ibid., 201.

2. Rereading the Book of Isaiah

1. Brevard S. Childs, *Introduction to the Old Testament as Scripture* (Philadelphia: Fortress Press, 1979) chap. 17; Ronald E. Clements, "The Unity of the Book of Isaiah," *Interpretation* 36 (1982) 117–29; and "Beyond Tradition-History: Deutero-Isaianic Development of First Isaiah's Themes," *JSOT* 31 (1985) 95–113.

2. Concerning a *seratim* approach to the texts, see David R. Blumenthal, *Facing the Abusing God: A Theology of Protest* (Louisville: Westminster John Knox, 1993) 47–54 and *passim.*

3. Harold Bloom, *A Map of Misreading* (Oxford: Oxford University Press, 1975).

4. Among the more important discussions of "the theology of the cross," see Alister E. McGrath, *Luther's Theology of the Cross: Martin Luther's Theological Breakthrough* (Oxford: Blackwell, 1985); Douglas John Hall, *Lighten Our Darkness: Toward an Indigenous Theology of the Cross* (Philadelphia: Westminster, 1976); and Jürgen Moltmann, *The Crucified God: The Cross of Christ as the Foundation and Criticism of Christian Theology* (San Francisco: Harper and Row, 1974).

5. Harold J. Grimm, ed., *Luther's Works* v. 31: *Career of the Reformer* I (Philadelphia: Muhlenberg Press, 1957) 52–53.

6. Ibid., 52–53, 68–69.

7. Jaroslav Pelikan, ed., *Luther's Works* v. 16: *Lectures on Isaiah, Chapters 1–39* (St. Louis: Concordia Publishing House, 1969) 65.

8. Ibid.

9. For a discussion of this text in what is likely its "original" sapient intention, see J. William Whedbee, *Isaiah and Wisdom* (Nashville: Abingdon, 1971) 80–110, and Hans Walter Wolff, *Amos the Prophet: The Man and His Background* (Philadelphia: Fortress Press, 1973) 17–34.

10. Karl Marx, *Texte aus der Rheinischen Zeitung von 1842/43 Mit*

Friedrich Engels' Artikeln im Anhang, ed. Hans Pelger (Trier: Karl-Marx-Haus, 1984). I am grateful to Elizabeth Morgan for helping me find this text.

11. Karl Marx, "Verhandlungen des 6. rheinischen Landtags. Von einem Rheinländer. Dritter Artikel: Debatten über das Holzdiebstahlsgesetz," in Marx, *Texte aus der Rheinischen Zeitung,* 78–109.

12. I am grateful to Arend Th. van Leeuwen, *Critique of Earth: The Second Series of the Gifford Lectures Entitled "Critique of Heaven and Earth"* (London: Lutterworth, 1974) 33–65, for his suggestive discussion of Marx's discussion of the legislation of wood. On these points, see van Leeuwen, *Critique of Earth,* 43–50.

13. van Leeuwen, *Critique of Earth,* 53.

14. Marx, "Debatten über das Holzdiebstahlsgesetz," 92.

15. Norman K. Gottwald, "Social Class and Ideology in Isaiah 40–55: An Eagletonian Reading," in *The Bible and Liberation: Political and Social Hermeneutics,* ed. Norman K. Gottwald and Richard S. Horsley, rev. ed. (Maryknoll: Orbis, 1993) 329–42; Walter Brueggemann, "Planned People/Planned Book?" in *Writing and Reading the Scroll of Isaiah: Studies of an Interpretive Tradition* I, ed. Craig C. Broyles and Craig A. Evans (Leiden: E. J. Brill, 1997) 19–37.

16. van Leeuwen, *Critique of Earth,* 58.

17. E. P. Thompson, *Customs in Common* (New York: The New Press, 1991).

18. Ibid., 175.

19. Ibid., 258 and *passim.*

20. Karl Polanyi, *The Great Transformation* (Boston: Beacon, 1957).

21. Extensive bibliography is offered by Peggy L. Day, ed., *Gender and Difference in Ancient Israel* (Minneapolis: Fortress Press, 1989), and more recently, Alice Ogden Bellis, *Helpmates, Harlots, and Heroes: Women's Stories in the Hebrew Bible* (Louisville: Westminster John Knox, 1994).

22. Phyllis Trible, *God and the Rhetoric of Sexuality* (OBT; Philadelphia: Fortress Press, 1978) 31–59.

23. Mayer I. Gruber, "The Motherhood of God in Second Isaiah," *RB* 90 (1983) 355, n. 15, refers to Derrick B. Jelliffe and E. F. Patrick Jelliffe, *Human Milk in the Modern World* (Oxford: Oxford University Press, 1978), with reference to the physiological issues that are pertinent.

24. Mayer I. Gruber, "The Motherhood of God in Second Isaiah," *RB* 90 (1983) 351–59.

25. Ibid., 356. Mention of "good mothers" suggests reference to the defining work of D. W. Winnicott. (See the first essay in this volume.)

26. Ibid., 359.

27. Such a procedure of course appeals to the dense understanding of symbol in the work of Paul Ricoeur.

28. Mary Gordon, *Men and Angels* (New York: Random House, 1985).

29. Ibid., 1, 209.

30. Ibid., 98.

31. Ibid., 113.

32. Ibid., 228.

33. Ibid., 231.

34. Paul D. Hanson, *The Dawn of Apocalyptic: The Historical and Sociological Roots of Jewish Apocalyptic* (Philadelphia: Fortress Press, 1975); Otto Plöger, *Theocracy and Eschatology* (Richmond: John Knox, 1968).

35. See David Jay Bercuson, *Confrontation at Winnipeg: Labour, Industrial Relations, and the General Strike* (Montreal: McGill-Queen's University Press, 1974).

36. See Kenneth McNaught, *A Prophet in Politics: A Biography of J. S. Woodsworth* (Toronto: University of Toronto Press, 1959), and A. Ross McCormack, *Reformers, Rebels, and Revolutionaries: The Western Canadian Radical Movement 1899–1919* (Toronto: University of Toronto Press, 1977) 77–97 and *passim*.

37. Arthur J. Griffin, "The Influence of the Old Testament Prophets upon the Life and Work of James Shaver Woodsworth" (thesis submitted to Union Theological College, Vancouver, B.C., 1951) 31–32. I am grateful to R. Gerald Hobbs for calling my attention to the case of Woodsworth, whose report to me was prompted by James Manley.

38. Gerhard von Rad, *Old Testament Theology II: The Theology of Israel's Prophetic Traditions* (San Francisco: Harper and Row, 1965), takes Isa. 43:18-19 as the opening motto for the volume. In the body of the volume he makes a great deal of the way in which 2 Isaiah opens a "new epoch" in the faith of Israel.

39. Childs, *Introduction*, 328–30. I regard Childs's suggestion, now followed by a number of scholars, as a brilliant interpretive move. It is my judgment, however, that the older interpretation that regards the "former things" as the Mosaic events is not as easily disposed of as Childs seems to suggest. See, for example, Jer. 23:7-8 as well as the allusion to Exodus in Isa. 43:18-19, on which see Bernhard W. Anderson, "Exodus Typology in Second Isaiah," in *Israel's Prophetic Heritage: Essays in Honor of James Muilenburg*, ed. Bernhard W. Anderson and Walter Harrelson (New York: Harper and Brothers, 1962) 177–95, and "Exodus and Covenant in Second Isaiah and Prophetic Tradition," in *Magnalia Dei, The Mighty Acts of God: Essays on the Bible and Archaeology in Memory of G. Ernest Wright*, ed. Frank Moore Cross et al. (Garden City, N.Y.: Doubleday, 1976) 339–60. See also the articles by A. Bentzen and C. North referenced by Childs.

40. Brian K. Blount, "Beyond the Boundaries: Cultural Perspective and the Interpretation of the New Testament" (Ph.D. Dissertation, Emory University, 1993). See also Theophus H. Smith, *Conjuring Culture: Biblical Formations of Black America* (Oxford: Oxford University Press, 1994). Smith proposes that the Bible was incessantly performative for the Black church community in conjuring an alternative culture.

41. Cf. James M. Washington, ed., *Testament of Hope: The Essential Speeches and Writings of Martin Luther King, Jr.* (San Francisco: Harper, 1986). More generally, see James H. Smylie, "On Jesus, Pharaohs, and the Chosen People: Martin Luther King as Biblical Interpreter and Humanist," *Interpretation* 24 (1970) 74–91.

42. Beverly J. Shamana, "Letting Go," in *Those Preachin' Women: Sermons by Black Women Preachers,* ed. Ella Pearson Mitchell (Valley Forge: Judson, 1985) 101–5. I am grateful to Marcia Riggs for leading me to this sermon.

43. See n. 39 above.

44. Shamana, "Letting Go," 102.

45. Ibid., 104.

46. Ibid., 103.

47. Jon D. Levenson, "Exodus and Liberation," in *The Hebrew Bible, the Old Testament, and Historical Criticism: Jews and Christians in Biblical Studies* (Louisville: Westminster John Knox, 1993) 127–59, vigorously opposes "liberationist supersessionism" (p. 157) whereby other groups, including African Americans, preempt the Jews as the subject of Exodus liberation. He does, however, allow that Martin Luther King Jr. responsibly made use of the Israelite tradition of liberation. See the different sort of comments by Paul M. van Buren, *A Theology of the Jewish-Christian Reality Part 2: A Christian Theology of the People Israel* (San Francisco: Harper and Row, 1983) 179–83.

48. Paul Ricoeur, "The Hermeneutical Function of Distanciation," in *From Text to Action: Essays in Hermeneutics* II (Evanston: Northwestern University Press, 1991) 83, observes that when the text becomes writing, it "opens itself to an unlimited series of readings, themselves situated in different sociocultural conditions." He asserts that "the text must be able, from the sociological as well as the psychological point of view, to 'decontextualize' itself in such a way that it can be 'recontextualized.'" It is this "recontextualization" that is the subject of our study. See also J. P. M. Walsh, "'Leave Out the Poetry' Reflections on the Teaching of Scripture," in *The Struggle Over the Past: Fundamentalism in the Modern World*, ed. William M. Shea, The Annual Publication of the College Theology Society 35 (1989) 317–26. For other cases of the "recontextualization" of Isaiah, see Philip Wheaton and Duane Shank, *Empire and the Word: Prophetic Parallels Between the Exilic Experience and Central America's Crisis* (EPICA Task Force, 1988). See the reference to Isa. 40:1-3 on p. 180 and to Isa. 25:8-9 on p. 262. See also Kornelis H. Miskotte, *When the Gods Are Silent* (New York: Harper and Row, 1967) 405–9, 415–22. Miskotte does not explicitly articulate a new context, but it is clearly implied in his eloquent testimony.

49. I make reference, of course, to Northrop Frye, *The Great Code: The Bible and Literature* (New York: Harcourt, Brace, 1982).

3. The Prophetic Word of God and History

1. On the problem in relation to the assumptions of modernity, see *God's Activity in the World: The Contemporary Problem*, ed. Owen C. Thomas (Chico: Scholars, 1983), and Werner E. Lemke, "Revelation Through History in Recent Biblical Theology," *Interpretation* 36 (January 1982) 34–46.

2. In this sentence I have moved from God's "action" to God's "speech." The two matters, act and word, are intimately linked with each other. James Barr in particular has taught us to pay attention to God's speech rather than God's actions.

3. The most helpful general discussion of modernity known to me is Stephen Toulmin, *Cosmopolis: The Hidden Agenda of Modernity* (New York: The Free Press, 1990).

4. I am glad to acknowledge the impact of George A. Lindbeck, *The Nature of Doctrine: Religion and Theology in a Postliberal Age* (Philadelphia: Westminster, 1984), upon my thinking. I have carried my own thinking in directions Lindbeck would not pursue, but his work has been enormously suggestive to me.

5. On this text and the theological trajectory that derives from it, see Walter Brueggemann, "'Impossibility' and Epistemology in the Faith Traditions of Abraham and Sarah (Genesis 18:1-15)," *ZAW* 94 (1982) 615–34, and Claus Westermann, *The Promises to the Fathers: Studies on the Patriarchal Narratives* (Philadelphia: Fortress Press, 1980) 11–12, 60–61.

6. There are, to be sure, many scholarly suggestions about sociohistorical antecedents to the existence of Israel. Without denying the importance or validity of those antecedents, it is unmistakable (a) that Israel is a genuine *novum* (new thing), no matter what historical critical judgments might be made, and (b) Israel understands itself as a *novum* in world history. On the continuities with Canaanite antecedents, see the several essays in *Ancient Israelite Religion, Essays in Honor of Frank Moore Cross*, ed. Patrick D. Miller et al. (Philadelphia: Fortress Press, 1987). On the theological, methodological issues of Israel as a theological *novum*, see M. Douglas Meeks, *Origins of the Theology of Hope* (Philadelphia: Fortress Press, 1974) 67–69 and *passim*.

7. Martin Buber, *Moses* (Atlantic Highlands, N.J.: Humanities Press International, 1988) 75–76. See the derivative discussions of Buber's theme by Emil Fackenheim, *God's Presence in History* (New York: Harper and Row, 1972).

8. Michael Walzer, *Exodus and Revolution* (New York: Basic Books, 1985).

9. On the human leadership of Moses, see Aaron Wildavsky, *The Nursing Father: Moses as a Political Leader* (Birmingham: University of Alabama Press, 1984).

10. On nontheological factors in understanding the prophets, concerning psychology, sociology, and anthropology respectively, see J. Lindblom, *Prophecy in Ancient Israel* (Philadelphia: Muhlenberg Press, 1962); Robert R. Wilson, *Prophecy and Society in Ancient Israel* (Philadelphia: Fortress

Press, 1980); and Thomas W. Overholt, *Channels of Prophecy: The Social Dynamics of Prophetic Activity* (Minneapolis: Fortress Press, 1989).

11. On Yahweh versus the idols, see Pablo Richard et al., *The Idols of Death and the God of Life: A Theology* (Maryknoll: Orbis Books, 1983). More generally on the interface of idolatry and ideology, see Walter Brueggemann, *Israel's Praise: Doxology against Idolatry and Ideology* (Philadelphia: Fortress Press, 1988).

12. On the dialectic of hurt and hope in the character and will of God, see Walter Brueggemann, "The Rhetoric of Hurt and Hope: Ethics Odd and Crucial," in *The Annual, Society of Christian Ethics,* ed. D. M. Yeager (Knoxville: Society of Christian Ethics, 1989) 73–92.

13. For summary statements of the crucial nature of hope for ancient Israel, see Walther Zimmerli, *Man and His Hope in the Old Testament* (SBT 2/20; Naperville: Alec R. Allenson, n.d.), and Hans Walter Wolff, *Anthropology of the Old Testament* (Philadelphia: Fortress Press, 1974) 149–55. More generally, see Donald E. Gowan, *Eschatology in the Old Testament* (Philadelphia: Fortress Press, 1986), and Walter Brueggemann, *Hopeful Imagination: Prophetic Voices in Exile* (Philadelphia: Fortress Press, 1986). It has been Jürgen Moltmann, *Theology of Hope: On the Ground and the Implications of a Christian Eschatology* (New York: Harper and Row, 1967), who has most fully considered the larger theological dimensions of the hope of ancient Israel, on which see also Meeks, *Origins of the Theology of Hope.*

14. In *Abiding Astonishment: Psalms, Modernity, and the Making of History* (Louisville: Westminster John Knox, 1991), I have argued that the impact of modernity upon the speech (and faith) of the church is not an irreversible cultural development, but the exercise of an option. This means that a recovery of such speech (and faith) that moves against modernity is also an option that can be chosen. Indeed, I have suggested that the "pre-rational" historical recital of ancient Israel may not be an "early" speech mode that was superseded by more "rational" thought, but it may be a subversive response to that more rational thought that was a mode of political domination. The point is an important one as a "postmodern" community of interpretation exercises an option in its mode of speech.

15. On the phrase, see Brueggemann, *Abiding Astonishment,* and the references to Martin Buber and Emil Fackenheim.

16. One dramatic example of the way in which technique can overcome speech is a recent incident in Germany. Protesting youths have systematically taken to writing graffiti as a social counterstatement. The government has countered by developing and utilizing a new chemical mix that has the capacity to erase the graffiti without damaging the surfaces on which they are written.

17. On the history-making word, see Walter Brueggemann, *Hope Within History* (Atlanta: John Knox, 1987) 49–71.

18. On this view of technology, see Jacques Ellul, *The Humiliation of the Word* (Grand Rapids: Eerdmans, 1985) and his more programmatic statement, *The Technological Society* (New York: Alfred A. Knopf, 1965).

19. Alasdair MacIntyre, *Whose Justice? Which Rationality?* (Notre Dame: University of Notre Dame Press, 1988) has provided a compelling analysis of the way in which every ethical "given" is in fact embedded in a narrative history that relativizes its claim and makes it available for criticism. Though MacIntyre does not explicitly dwell on the claims of a technological ideology, the categories of his argument are pertinent for such a critique.

20. See Walter Brueggemann, "Living Toward a Vision: Grief in the Midst of Technique," in *Hope within History*, 72–91.

21. In "Vine and Fig Tree: A Case Study in Imagination and Criticism," *CBQ* 43 (1981) 188–204, I have reflected specifically on the way in which Israel's prophets engaged in the twin tasks of criticism and imagination of an alternative.

22. Francis Fukuyama, *The End of History and the Last Man* (New York: The Free Press, 1992). What Fukuyama prefers to judge "the end of history" is given a much more discerning, ambiguous assessment by Theodore H. von Laue, *The World Revolution of Westernization: The Twentieth Century in Global Perspective* (New York: Oxford University Press, 1987).

23. On this text, see Gerhard von Rad, *Wisdom in Israel*, trans. J. D. Martin (Nashville: Abingdon, 1972). Von Rad writes:

> Its aim is, rather, to put a stop to the erroneous concept that a guarantee of success was to be found simply in practicing human wisdom and in making preparations. Man must always keep himself open to the activity of God, an activity which completely escapes all calculation, for between the putting into practice of the most reliable wisdom and that which then actually takes place, there always lies a great unknown (101). They also knew that the world is encompassed within the incalculable mystery of God (234). For this reason, all objects of human knowledge were on the one hand knowable and, on the other, subject to a divine mystery to which God could at any time recall them, thus concealing them from man (310).

4. The "Baruch Connection": Reflections on Jeremiah 43:1-7

1. William L. Holladay, *Jeremiah 1: A Commentary on the Book of the Prophet Jeremiah, Chapters 1–25* (Hermeneia; Philadelphia: Fortress Press, 1986); *Jeremiah 2: A Commentary on the Book of the Prophet Jeremiah, Chapters 26–52* (Hermeneia; Minneapolis: Fortress Press, 1989); and Robert

P. Carroll, *Jeremiah, A Commentary* (OTL; Philadelphia: Westminster, 1986).

2. In addition to his commentary, see Robert P. Carroll, *From Chaos to Covenant: Prophecy in the Book of Jeremiah* (New York: Crossroad, 1981).

3. The work of Holladay and Carroll, respectively, coincides with the work of Helga Weippert, *Die Prosareden des Jeremiabuches* (BZAW 132; Berlin: de Gruyter, 1973), and Winfried Thiel, *Die deuteronomistische Redaktion von Jer. 1–25* (WMANT 41; Neukirchen-Vluyn: Neukirchener Verlag, 1973); *Die deuteronomistiche Redaktion von Jer. 26–52* (WMANT 52; Neukirchen-Vluyn: Neukirchener Verlag, 1981).

4. A. R. Diamond, *The Confessions of Jeremiah in Context: Scenes of Prophetic Drama* (JSOTSup 45; Sheffield: JSOT, 1987); Kathleen M. O'Connor, *The Confessions of Jeremiah: Their Interpretation and Role in Chapters 1–25* (SBLDS 94; Atlanta: Scholars, 1988), and Mark S. Smith, *The Laments of Jeremiah in Their Context: A Literary and Redactional Study of Jeremiah 11–20* (Atlanta: Scholars, 1990).

5. William S. McKane, *A Critical and Exegetical Commentary on Jeremiah* I (ICC; Edinburgh: T. & T. Clark, 1986) l–lxxxiii.

6. Brevard S. Childs, *Introduction to the Old Testament as Scripture* (Philadelphia: Fortress Press, 1979) 345–47.

7. Ronald E. Clements, "Patterns in the Prophetic Canon," in *Canon and Authority: Essays in Old Testament Religion and Theology,* ed. George W. Coats and Burke O. Long (Philadelphia: Fortress Press, 1977) 42–55.

8. Christopher R. Seitz, *Theology in Conflict: Reactions to the Exile in the Book of Jeremiah* (BZAW 176; Berlin: de Gruyter, 1989).

9. On recent developments in "canonical criticism," see Gerald T. Sheppard, "Canonical Criticism," *The Anchor Bible Dictionary* ed. David Noel Freedman et al. (New York: Doubleday, 1992) vol. 1, 861–66.

10. On the matter of the Masoretic Text, see J. Gerald Janzen, *Studies in the Text of Jeremiah* (HSM 6; Cambridge: Harvard University Press, 1973).

11. On the "Baruch source," see the programmatic discussion of G. Wanke, *Untersuchungen zur sogenannten Baruchschrift* (BZAW 122; Berlin: de Gruyter, 1971).

12. Holladay, *Jeremiah 2,* 215–16 and *passim.*

13. Carroll, *Jeremiah,* 665, 722–24 and *passim.* See also Carroll, *From Chaos to Covenant,* 151.

14. J. Andrew Dearman, "My Servants the Scribes: Composition and Context in Jeremiah 36," *JBL* 109 (1990) 404, n. 2.

15. Ibid. On the ideological dimension of Deuteronomic theology, see Patricia Dutcher-Walls, "The Social Location of the Deuteronomists: A Sociological Study of Factional Politics in Late Pre-exilic Judah," *JSOT* 52 (1991) 77–94, and Norman K. Gottwald, "Social Class as an Analytic and Hermeneutical Category in Biblical Studies," *JBL* 112 (1993) 12–13 and *passim.*

16. Seitz, *Theology in Conflict,* provides a complete review of the disputes, understanding them as rival claims for authority among competing exilic communities.

17. Ibid., 52–57. See Jay A. Wilcoxen, "The Political Background of Jeremiah's Temple Sermon," in *Scripture in History and Theology: Essays in Honor of J. Coert Rylaarsdom,* ed. Arthur J. Merrill and Thomas W. Overholt, PTMS 17 (Pittsburgh: Pickwick, 1977) 151–66.

18. See Thomas W. Overholt, *The Threat of Falsehood: A Study in the Theology of the Book of Jeremiah* (SBT 16; London: SCM, 1970), and more generally James L. Crenshaw, *Prophetic Conflict: Its Effect Upon Israelite Religion* (BZAW 124; Berlin: de Gruyter, 1971) 62–90.

19. See also chapters 27–28.

20. Though the wording is not the same, the mood evoked is parallel to that of the so-called Scythian Songs of chapters 4–6. The stylized language of v. 11 is equivalent to that of 15:2, which suggests that the curses to be brought against Jerusalem are now extended to Egypt. See also the description in chapter 46 of the damage to be worked against Egypt. At least in the prose interpretive comments of vv. 2, 13, and 26, the agent of that devastation is Nebuchadnezzar. Thus our verses reflect a view championed elsewhere in the book of Jeremiah, and by the use of the same sort of rhetoric extend the work "from the North" even against Egypt.

21. On the "return to Egypt," see Richard Elliott Friedman, "From Egypt to Egypt: Dtr1 and Dtr2," *Traditions in Transition,* ed. Baruch Halpern and Jon D. Levenson (Winona Lake, Ind.: Eisenbrauns, 1981) 167–92. See also D. J. Reimer, "Concerning Return to Egypt: Deuteronomy xvii 16 and xxviii 68 Reconsidered" in *Studies in the Pentateuch,* ed. J. A. Emerton (SVT 41: Leiden, 1990) 217–29.

22. By "innocence" I do not mean ignorance or naivete. Rather, I mean that the poetic tradition of Jeremiah sought to cut underneath specific political recommendations to more elemental theological matters, even though those theological matters had important, if unspecific, political implications. It is possible to see in the recent work of Vaclav Havel in Czechoslovakia something of a parallel, when Havel was an artistic figure in protest and before he became politically engaged as a party figure and an office holder. For example, in his letter to Gustav Husak, "Dear Mr. Husak," in *Open Letters: Selected Writings 1965–1990* (New York: Vintage Books, 1992) 52–83, Havel makes no specific political urging but simply makes evident the destructive power of falsehood in the deceptiveness of the government. Such an exposé has important political spin-off, but Havel at that point does not articulate it. The evolution of Havel's career from artist to politician may help us to see the very different role of the artist in the political process.

No doubt Jeremiah's commitment to the radicalness of the Mosaic tradition and the resultant criticism of dynastic theology have important political spin-off. The more concrete statements of that political spin-off, however, are expressed in prose, much of which evidences Deuteronomic recasting, that is, articulation of a more concretely political kind. I do not suggest that Jeremiah is free of "ideology," for his covenantal Yahwism is an ideology. Indeed, Paul Ricoeur, *From Text to Action: Essays in Hermeneutics* II, trans. Kathleen Blamey and John B. Thompson (Evanston: Northwestern University Press, 1991) 207, cf. 254, is surely correct in concluding that there is "no place that is completely outside of ideology." Such an advocacy as that of Jeremiah, however, is of a different sort from the more blatant political practice of the Deuteronomists, whose own benefit in their advocacy is relatively transparent. In a broad sense, every advocacy is "ideology," but not all "ideologies" serve "distortion," which is grounded in pragmatic interest. It is not easy to identify pragmatic interest in Jeremiah's "ideology." Thus, while the ideology of Jeremiah is "integrating," it is not "distorting" in the same sense as is that of the Deuteronomists.

23. On the "use" of the tradition by the pro-Babylonians, see Else Kragelund Holt, "The Chicken and the Egg—Or: Was Jeremiah a Member of the Deuteronomist Party?" *JSOT* 44 (1989) 102–22.

24. Carroll, *Jeremiah*, 723, 724, 740, 742, uses the term. It is probable, however, that Marx's understanding of ideology concerns not only "distortion" but already anticipates the later notion of ideology as a "strategy of containment." See Fredric Jameson, *The Political Unconscious: Narrative as a Socially Symbolic Act* (Ithaca: Cornell University Press, 1981) 49–58, on the notion of "ideology" in relation to "totality."

Michele Barrett, *The Politics of Truth: From Marx to Foucault* (Stanford: Stanford University Press, 1991) has subjected the Marxian notion of ideology to careful critical review. In light of the work of Gramsci, Lacan, Althusser, and Foucault, the Marxian notion of ideology is shown to be enormously complex and problematic, if not contradictory. The issue that concerns Barrett is the interrelation of "class setting" for ideology and a more general notion of "mystification" without reference to class situation. Barrett concludes:

> There is, in my view, a useful set of meanings that the term ideology can capture well; they cluster around processes of mystification. The retrievable core of meaning of the term ideology is precisely this: discursive and significatory mechanisms that may occlude, legitimate, naturalise or universalise in a variety of different ways but can all be said to mystify. In such a usage, the term ideology is clearly a general term referring to mystification: it refers to a function of mechanism but is not tied to any particular content, nor to any particular agent or interest. On this definition, ideology is not tied to any one presumed cause, or logic, of misrepresentation; it refers to a process of mystification, or misrepresentation, whatever its dynamic. (pp. 166–67)

Such a conclusion is consistent with the usage of the term "ideology" in this chapter. The conclusion of Barrett suggests, as concerns Scripture study, that the label "ideology" can as well apply to so-called "objective" or "neutral" readings as those that attend to the theological claims of the text.

25. Carroll, *Jeremiah*, 242.

26. Ibid., 244.

27. Ibid., 246.

28. Thus Marx asserts: "The criticism of heaven is thus transformed into the criticism of earth, the criticism of religion into the criticism of law, and the criticism of theology into the criticism of politics." Cf. David McLellan, *The Thought of Karl Marx: An Introduction* (New York: Macmillan, 1971) 22.

29. On these categories in relation to the Jeremiah tradition, see Henri Mottu, "Jeremiah vs. Hananiah: Ideology and Truth in Old Testament Prophecy," in *The Bible and Liberation: Political and Social Hermeneutics*, ed. Norman K. Gottwald (Maryknoll: Orbis Books, 1983) 235–51.

30. Clifford Geertz stands at the forefront of those who seek to reposition "objectivist" social science to overcome the presumed contrast between "real" and "religious." Thus Geertz ("Blurred Genres: The Refiguration of Social Thought," *The American Scholar* 49 [1980] 178) writes, ". . . a challenge is being mounted to some of the central assumptions of mainstream social science. The strict separation of theory and data, the 'brute fact' idea; the effort to create a formal vocabulary of analysis purged of all subjective reference, the 'ideal language' idea; and the claim to moral neutrality and the Olympian view, the 'God's truth' idea—none of these can prosper when explanation comes to be regarded as a matter of connecting action to its sense rather than behavior to its determinants." And in "Religion as a Cultural System," in *Reader in Comparative Religion: An Anthropological Approach*, ed. William Lessa and Evon Vogt (New York: Harper and Row, 1965) 215, Geertz asserts that our sense of God or the "really real" colors our "sense of the reasonal, the practical, the humane and the moral." See also the discussion of Judith Plaskow, *Standing Again at Sinai: Judaism from a Feminist Perspective* (San Francisco: Harper and Row, 1990) 126.

31. See the shrewd argument of Marion Ann Taylor, "Jeremiah 45: The Problem of Placement," *JSOT* 37 (1987) 79–98. Taylor sees in the chapter a promise to the person of Baruch, but the larger intention, indicated by placement, is a massive announcement of judgment, that is, "the fourth year of Jehoiachim."

32. Apart from the prose commentary, the destroyer in chapter 46 is of course unnamed. The ominous threat created by the rhetoric is parallel to that of the so-called Scythian Songs, for which the intended subject seems deliberately opaque. On the latter, see the papers by Henri Cazelles, Brevard S. Childs, and C. F. Whitley in *A Prophet to the Nations: Essays in Jeremiah Studies*, ed. Leo G. Perdue and Brian W.

Kovacs (Winona Lake, Ind.: Eisenbrauns, 1984) 129–49, 151–61, and 163–73.

33. On this programmatic set of words, see Carroll, *From Chaos to Covenant*, 55–58; and Prescott H. Williams Jr. "Living Toward the Acts of the Savior-Judge: A Study of Eschatology in the Book of Jeremiah," *Austin Seminary Bulletin* (1979) 13–39.

34. Carroll, *Jeremiah*, 240. Carroll moves almost without pause from "ideology" (by which he seems to mean distortion) to realpolitik. Indeed, in Carroll's presentation, there seems to be no third alternative to ideology and realpolitik, thus by definition precluding the attribution of any seriousness to the assertions of Jeremiah or what purport to be the faith claims of the Baruch community. They are in principle nullified.

35. Fredric Jameson, *The Political Unconscious: Narrative as a Socially Symbolic Act*, 289.

36. Paul Ricoeur, *Lectures on Ideology and Utopia* (New York: Columbia University Press, 1986) 251.

37. Paul Ricoeur, "The Creativity of Language," in *A Ricoeur Reader: Reflection and Imagination*, ed. Mario J. Valdes (Toronto: University of Toronto Press, 1991) 475.

38. Dearman, "My Servants the Scribes," 408–21, identifies the generations of this family and situates them in the work of Deuteronomic scribal circles.

39. This judgment of course fails to account for chapter 52. A concern to identify the canonical intention of this chapter lies beyond the scope of this chapter and remains for further consideration.

40. On the notion of "plans" in these texts, see Walter Brueggemann, "Genesis 1:15-21: A Theological Exploration" in *Congress Volume, Salamanca 1983*, ed. J. A. Emerton (SVT 36; Leiden: E. J. Brill, 1985) 40–53.

41. Whether this anticipation of a return home is "utopian" or more "ideological" depends upon the interpreter's extrapolation. There is, however, no built-in tilt toward ideology. For that reason, I read with the grain of the text. There is a temptation, given the reader's propensity for ideology, to read the text as ideology, even when the text intends otherwise.

42. The Scythian Songs have been intensely studied. See n. 29. Because of scholarly attention to form analysis, it is conventional to study the Oracles Against the Nations in chapters 46–51 as though they are completely separated from the earlier poetry. Attention to canonical intentionality requires and permits breaking out of such a "form"-controlled analysis. The result is a fresh field of enquiry concerning the intertextual relation of the earlier and later poetry.

43. On the theme of "no mercy," see especially Isa. 46–47. See Walter Brueggemann, "At the Mercy of Babylon: A Subversive Rereading of the Empire," *JBL* 110 (1991) 3–22.

44. I am grateful to Tim Beal for his suggestions concerning this chapter.

5. The Scandal and Liberty of Particularity

1. Peter L. Berger and Thomas Luckmann, *The Social Construction of Reality: A Treatise in the Sociology of Knowledge* (Garden City, N.Y.: Anchor Books/Doubleday, 1967).

2. I am of course aware that internally there were certainly hegemonic groups that prevailed. By focusing on the impact of the international empires, I do not overlook internal domination. I assume that patterns of domination are roughly the same, whether by external or internal agents.

3. On this motif in Israelite perspective, see Donald E. Gowan, *When Man Becomes God: Humanism and Hubris in the Old Testament* (PTMS 6; Pittsburgh: Pickwick, 1975).

4. Norman K. Gottwald, "A Hypothesis about Social Class in Monarchic Israel in the Light of Contemporary Studies of Social Class and Social Stratification," in *The Hebrew Bible in Its Social World and in Ours* (Atlanta: Scholars, 1993) 139–64, has offered an analysis of the realities of class in the formation of the monarchy.

5. Theodore H. von Laue, *The World Revolution of Westernization: The Twentieth Century in Global Perspective* (New York: Oxford University Press, 1987); Charles Reich, *Opposing the System* (New York: Random House, 1995).

6. See R. Frankena, "The Vassal-Treaties of Esarhaddon and the Dating of Dt," *Oudtestamentische Studien* 14 (1965) 122–54; Dennis J. McCarthy, *Treaty and Covenant: A Study in Form in the Ancient Oriental Documents and in the Old Testament* rev.ed. (Analecta Biblica 21A; Rome: Biblical Institute, 1978); and Moshe Weinfeld, *Deuteronomy and the Deuteronomic School* (Oxford: Clarendon, 1972).

7. John Van Seters, *Abraham in History and Tradition* (New Haven: Yale University Press, 1975).

8. See Walter Brueggemann, "A Poem of Summons (Is. 55:1-3)? A Narrative of Resistance (Dan. 1:1-21)," in *Schopfung und Befreiung,* ed. Rainer Albertz et al. (Stuttgart: Calwer Verlag, 1989) 126–36.

9. Jeffries M. Hamilton, *Social Justice and Deuteronomy: The Case of Deuteronomy 15* (SBLDS 136; Atlanta: Scholars, 1992); Moshe Weinfeld, *Social Justice in Ancient Israel and in the Ancient Near East* (Minneapolis: Fortress Press, 1995).

10. See David Daube, *The Exodus Pattern in the Bible* (Westport: Greenwood, 1979). Daube has suggested links between the year of release and the Exodus narrative.

11. Gottwald, "Prolegomenon: How My Mind Has Changed or Remained the Same," in *The Hebrew Bible in Its Social World and In Ours* 25, has most recently adopted the term "communitarian" to characterize the vision of revolutionary Israel. Gottwald employed this word after his earlier term, *egalitarian,* was roundly criticized.

12. See Walter Brueggemann, "Reflections on Biblical Understandings of

Property," in *A Social Reading of the Old Testament: Prophetic Approaches to Israel's Communal Life* (Minneapolis: Fortress Press, 1994) 276–84.

13. On the use of the term "triage" in such a way, see Richard L. Rubenstein, *After Auschwitz: History, Theology and Contemporary Judaism*, 2nd ed. (Baltimore: Johns Hopkins University Press, 1992). Zygmunt Bauman, *Modernity and the Holocaust* (Ithaca: Cornell University Press, 1992), has shown how the Holocaust was a most modernist approach to the problem of surplus people.

14. See Robert G. Hall, "Circumcision," in *Anchor Bible Dictionary*, ed. David Noel Freedman (New York: Doubleday, 1992) vol. 1, 1028–29.

15. "A Prayer for the Continuity of American Jewish Life," *New York Times* (September 6, 1996).

16. See Walter Harrelson, *From Fertility Cult to Worship: A Reassessment for the Modern Church of the Worship of Ancient Israel* (Garden City, N.Y.: Doubleday, 1969).

17. Jacob Neusner, *The Enchantments of Judaism: Rites of Transformation From Birth through Death* (New York: Basic Books, 1987) 211–16 and *passim*.

6. Always in the Shadow of the Empire

1. H. Richard Niebuhr, *Christ and Culture* (New York: Harper and Brothers, 1951). Niebuhr's classic presentation still provides a way into the subject, although the book is now criticized, especially because the notions of gospel and culture in the book are both monolithic, without taking into account the reality that the gospel takes many forms and culture is inevitably pluralistic in any context. See Robert E. Webber, *The Church in the World: Opposition, Tension or Transformation?* (Grand Rapids: Zondervan, 1986) 261–78.

2. See Charles Reich, *Opposing the System* (New York: Random House, 1995), and Richard J. Barnet, *The Global War against the Poor* (Washington: The Servant Leadership School, n.d.).

3. There is no doubt, according to current scholarly judgment, a deep and pervasive tension between the *practice* of Israelite religion on the ground and the *ideology* that is imposed on the Old Testament, which comes to be "normative" for the Old Testament. It is likely that it is the tension itself that is the subject of our study, rather than choosing one or the other of these alternatives. For a comprehensive discussion of the matter, see Rainer Albertz, *A History of Israelite Religion in the Old Testament Period I: From the Beginnings to the End of the Monarchy,* trans. J. Bowden (OTL; Louisville: Westminster John Knox, 1994); *A History of Israelite Religion in the Old Testament Period II: From the Exile to the Maccabees* (OTL; Louisville: Westminster John Knox, 1994).

The actual terms we use for this process are curious. For a very long time, "syncretism" has been a pejorative term bespeaking inappropriate "mixing." "Synergism," however, concerns mobilization of energies in a positive effort.

4. On the "mythic" component in this "historical narrative, see Frank Moore Cross, "The Cultus of the Israelite League," in *Canaanite Myth and Hebrew Epic: Essays in the History of the Religion of Israel* (Cambridge: Harvard University Press, 1973) 79–144.

5. See Walter Brueggemann, "The Exodus Narrative as Israel's Articulation of Faith Development," in *Hope within History* (Atlanta: John Knox, 1987) 7–26.

6. Frank Crüsemann, *The Torah: Theology and Social History of Old Testament Law* (Minneapolis: Fortress Press, 1996) 57, nicely makes the case that "Sinai is, however, a utopian place. It is temporally and physically outside state authority." That is, Sinai stands behind and outside every historical explanation and is the ultimate source of command.

7. The "down side" of the Torah tradition is made clear, for example, by Carolyn Pressler, *The View of Women Found in the Deuteronomic Family Laws* (BZAW 216; Berlin: de Gruyter, 1993), who demonstrates that the laws are rigidly patriarchal in orientation.

8. See the fine study by Marva J. Dawn, *Keeping the Sabbath Wholly: Ceasing, Resting, Embracing, Feasting* (Grand Rapids: Eerdmans, 1989).

9. See Moshe Weinfeld, *Social Justice in Ancient Israel and in the Ancient Near East* (Minneapolis: Fortress Press, 1995), who demonstrates that justice in the Old Testament pivots around the "sabbatic principle" expressed in Sabbath, the year of release, and the year of jubilee. On the latter, see Maria Harris, *Proclaim Jubilee! A Spirituality for the Twenty-First Century* (Louisville: Westminster John Knox, 1996).

10. On this remarkable text, see Hans Walter Wolff, "The Kerygma of the Yahwist," *Interpretation* 20 (1966) 152 and *passim*, and Walter Brueggemann," Subversive Modes of Blessing," (forthcoming).

11. On this text, see Marvin L. Chaney, "You Shall Not Covet Your Neighbor's House," *Pacific Theological Review* 15.2 (Winter 1982) 3–13.

12. On the term "Canaanite" as an ideological marker, see Niels Peter Lemche, *The Canaanites and Their Land: The Tradition of the Canaanites* (JSOTSup 110; Sheffield: JSOT Press, 1991).

13. See Ernest W. Nicholson, *God and His People: Covenant and Theology in the Old Testament* (New York: Oxford University Press, 1986).

14. On this text, see Jeffries M. Hamilton, *Social Justice and Deuteronomy: The Case of Deuteronomy 15* (Atlanta: Scholars Press, 1992).

15. On Israel amid the Babylonians, see Daniel L. Smith, *The Religion of the Landless: The Social Context of the Babylonian Exile* (Indianapolis: Meyer Stone, 1989).

16. On the Priestly material, see the review by Robert B. Coote and David Robert Ord in *In the Beginning: Creation and the Priestly History* (Minneapolis: Fortress Press, 1991).

17. Generally on the theological problem of presence in the Old Testament, see Samuel L. Terrien, *The Elusive Presence: Toward a New Biblical Theology* (San Francisco: Harper and Row, 1978). On the Priestly materials, see especially pp. 161–226.

18. One must of course notice the irony that this vigorous form and concern for purity and separatism is *funded* by the Persians. One might expect that a movement for purity and separation would insist upon the avoidance of such external funding, as in the case of the "Three Self" movement in the Chinese church. But alas (cf. Neh. 9:37)!

19. See the magisterial study of the subject by Martin Hengel, *Judaism and Hellenism*, trans. J. Bowden (Philadelphia: Fortress Press, 1974). The "Maccabean revolt," whatever its intention or historical shape, stands as the definitional marker for resistance to Hellenization and any other such option for accommodation.

20. See Reich, *Opposing the System;* Theodore H. von Laue, *The World Revolution of Westernization: The Twentieth Century in Global Perspective* (New York: Oxford University Press, 1987); and less directly, Jacques Ellul, *The Technological Society,* trans. J. Wilkinson (New York: Knopf, 1965).

21. Jacob Neusner, *The Enchantments of Judaism: Rites of Transformation from Birth through Death* (New York: Basic Books, 1987).

22. Neusner, *The Enchantments of Judaism,* 214, concludes, "We are Jews through the power of our imagination."

7. Exodus in the Plural (Amos 9:7)

I am pleased to offer this chapter to Shirley Guthrie in gratitude and appreciation for his generous ways of collegiality.

1. A popular and fair example of this liberal developmentalism is to be found in Harry Emerson Fosdick, *A Guide to Understanding the Bible: The Development of Ideas within the Old and New Testaments* (London: SCM Press, 1938).

2. On the scholarly debate on monotheism, see especially Mark S. Smith, *The Early History of God: Yahweh and the Other Deities in Ancient Israel* (San Francisco: Harper and Row, 1990), and Patrick D. Miller, "Israelite Religion," *The Hebrew Bible and Its Modern Interpreters,* ed. Douglas A. Knight and Gene M. Tucker (Philadelphia: Fortress Press, 1985) 210–37. Particular attention should be paid to the work of Bernhard Lang cited there. James A. Sanders, "Adaptable for Life: The Nature and Function of Canon," in *From Sacred Story to Sacred Text: Canon as Paradigm* (Philadelphia: Fortress Press, 1987) 9–39, has nicely used the phrase "monotheizing tendency," by which he means that Israel is "soft" on a full monotheism. I understand my comments here not to be opposed to those of Sanders but to state the other side of a dialectic that is critical of absolutism.

There was as well a pluralizing tendency, albeit a minority report, among those who formulated canon.

3. The translation of Deut. 6:4 concerning Yahweh as "one" or as "only" is not obvious. See Patrick D. Miller, *Deuteronomy* (Interpretation; Louisville: John Knox, 1990) 97–104; J. Gerald Janzen, "On the Most Important Word in the Shema," *VT* 37 (1987) 280–300; and S. Dean McBride Jr., "The Yoke of the Kingdom: Exposition of Deuteronomy 6:4-5," *Interpretation* 27 (1973) 273–306.

4. I use the awkward term "onlyness" in order to flag that the use of "monotheism" is a particularly performative notion in scholarship.

5. I intend by this term to refer not only to theological monotheism but also to its allied claim of "mono-people."

6. Rainer Albertz, *A History of Israelite Religion in the Old Testament Period, Volume I: From the Beginnings to the End of the Monarchy,* OTL (Louisville: Westminster John Knox, 1994) 105–38. See also Albertz, "Der Ort des Monotheismus in der israelitischen Religionsgeschichte," in *Ein Gott Allein? JHWH-Verehrung und biblischer Monotheismus im Kontext der israelitischen und altorientalischen Religionsgeschichte,* ed. Walter Dietrich und M. A. Klopfenstein (Freiburg: Universtätsverlag, 1994) 77–96.

7. C. J. Labuschagne, *The Incomparability of Yahweh in the Old Testament* (Leiden: Brill, 1966) has fully reviewed the formulae of incomparability.

8. On the "Yahweh alone" party, see Morton Smith, *Palestinian Parties and the Politics That Shaped the Old Testament* (New York: Columbia University Press, 1971). On the crucial nature of Deuteronomy, see Lothar Perlitt, *Bundestheologie im Alten Testament* (WMANT 36; Neukirchen-Vluyn: Neukirchener, 1969), and the summary of the discussion by Ernest Nicholson, *God and His People: Covenant and Theology in the Old Testament* (Oxford: Clarendon, 1986).

9. Gerhard von Rad, *Studies in Deuteronomy,* trans. D. Stalker (SBT 9; London: SCM, 1953) 74–91. The same material is reiterated by von Rad, *Old Testament Theology* I (San Francisco: Harper and Row, 1962) 334–47.

10. Here I make no claim for the historicity of the account offered by the Deuteronomists of Josiah. Even if the account is fiction, it evidences the determination of this tradition to hold together Mosaic Torah and royal claims.

11. The peculiar function of "name theology" was first contributed in contemporary scholarship by von Rad, *Studies in Deuteronomy* 37–44. It has now been more fully explicated in relation to other theologies of presence by Tryggve N. D. Mettinger, *The Dethronement of Sabaoth: Studies in the Shem and Kabod Theologies* (Coniectanea Biblica, Old Testament Series 18; Lund: C. W. K. Gleerup, 1982) 38–79. One important example of name theology is evident in 1 Kings 8. In vv. 12-13, we are offered an unqualified notice of material presence in the temple, which is promptly protested in vv. 27-30, which are evidently an expression of the theology of name.

12. I take the terms "developmental" and "ideological" to contrast in a

specific and accurate way the dominant horizons of classical nineteenth-century scholarship and our present situation. Part of the work of Old Testament theology is now to move our understanding of texts out of a developmental pattern and into an awareness of the ideological dimension of texts.

13. Here I make no historical assumptions about Amos but seek to work with the text as it comes to us. See n. 10.

14. Of course the term "orthodoxy" is an anachronism here. But the confrontation in Amos 7:10-17, between the prophet and the priest who is the chaplain of the king, suggests that there was an authorized interpretation of matters that would tolerate no deviation. Thus the term is not remote from the actual conflict. On the text in Amos 7:10-17, see Peter R. Ackroyd, "A Judgment Narrative Between Kings and Chronicles? An Approach to Amos 7:9-17," in *Canon and Authority: Essays in Old Testament Religion and Theology*, ed. George W. Coats and Burke O. Long (Philadelphia: Fortress Press, 1977) 71–87.

15. On this strategy in Amos, see Katherine J. Dell, "The Misuse of Forms in Amos," *VT* 45 (1995) 45–61.

16. The oracle against Judah is often regarded as late in the text. This judgment, however, has no bearing on the argument I am seeking to make.

17. Francis I. Anderson and David Noel Freedman, *Amos: A New Translation with Introduction and Commentary* (AB 15A; New York: Doubleday, 1989) 867–70.

18. Max E. Polley, *Amos and the Davidic Empire: A Socio-Historical Approach* (New York: Oxford University Press, 1989), in part following John Mauchline, has proposed that the book of Amos is committed to a Davidic political vision of reality.

19. The text of course reads "sons," but the inclusive rendering does not at all change the intention of those who are addressed.

20. It is not clear that the contrast means to accent the matter of race, that is, the Ethiopians are blacks. If this dimension is intended, then of course the radicalness of the contrast is even more powerful.

21. Dell, "The Misuse of Forms in Amos," 58–59, comments: "Here again Amos is taking a familiar formulation and filling it with a surprising and devastating new content in a fresh context."

22. John Barton, *Amos's Oracles Against the Nations: A Study of Amos 1:3–2:5* (Cambridge: Cambridge University Press, 1980) 37, following Hans Walter Wolff, takes the phrasing as a quotation of a familiar formula of Israel.

23. Ibid., 37.

24. On the relation of Genesis to Exodus, see R. W. L. Moberly, *The Old Testament of the Old Testament: Patriarchal Narratives and Mosaic Yahwism* (OBT; Minneapolis: Fortress Press, 1992).

25. See my more extended comments on this passage in Brueggemann, "Exodus," in *The New Interpreter's Bible* I, ed. Leander E. Keck et al. (Nashville: Abingdon, 1994) 705–7.

26. There are many accounts of various "hidden histories." The one with which I am most familiar is Barbara Brown Zigmund, ed., *Hidden Histories in the United Church of Christ* I and II (Cleveland: Pilgrim, 1984, 1989).

27. The first step in such an initiative is voicing pain that then turns to energy, precisely what the slaves in Egypt did. On that process in contemporary life, see Rebecca S. Chopp, *The Power to Speak: Feminism, Language and God* (New York: Crossroad, 1991); Judith Herman, *Trauma and Recovery: The Aftermath of Violence—From Domestic Abuse to Political Terror* (New York: Basic Books, 1993); and Elaine Scarry, *The Body in Pain: The Making and Unmaking of the World* (New York: Oxford University Press, 1987).

28. On this formula, see Rudolf Smend, *Die Bundesformel* (Theologische Studien 68; Zürich: EVZ, 1963).

29. On the crucial nature of a core of constancy in the character of Yahweh, see Dale Patrick, *The Rendering of God in the Old Testament* (OBT; Philadelphia: Fortress Press, 1981).

30. On a characteristic tension between the Deuteronomists and Amos, see Frank Crüsemann, "Kritik an Amos im deuteronomistischen Geschichtswerk: Erwägungen zu 2. Könige 14:27," in *Probleme biblischer Theologie: Gerhard von Rad Zum 70. Geburtstag,* ed. Hans Walter Wolff (München: Chr. Kaiser, 1971) 57–63.

31. For one example of such an exercise in nostalgia, see Allan D. Bloom, *The Closing of the American Mind: How Higher Education Has Failed Democracy and Impoverished the Souls of Today's Students* (New York: Simon and Schuster, 1987).

32. Jon D. Levenson, "Exodus and Liberation," in *The Hebrew Bible, The Old Testament, and Historical Criticism: Jews and Christians in Biblical Studies* (Louisville: Westminster John Knox, 1993) 127–59, reprinted from *Horizons in Biblical Theology* 131 (1991).

33. Ibid., 159.

34. Jacob Neusner, *Children of the Flesh, Children of the Promise: A Rabbi Talks with Paul* (Cleveland: Pilgrim, 1995).

35. Maurice Wiles, *Christian Theology and Interreligious Dialogue* (Philadelphia: Trinity Press International, 1992) 76.

36. Thus in the right moment, both activities are proper and indispensable. One can see a parallel in the presentation of Christopher Bollas, *Cracking Up: The Work of Unconscious Experience* (London: Routledge, 1995). Bollas writes:

> This freedom is found in the necessary opposition between the part of us that finds truth by uniting disparate ideas (i.e., "condensation") and the part of us that finds the truth by breaking up these unities. (p. 3)

This seems to me a close parallel to monotheizing and pluralizing.

37. Karl Barth, *The Word of God and the Word of Man,* trans. D. Horton (London: Hodder and Stoughton, 1928) 325–26.

38. Klaus Scholder, *A Requiem for Hitler and Other New Perspectives on the German Church Struggle* (London: SCM, 1989) 44.

39. James M. Robinson, "The Historicality of Biblical Language," in *The Old Testament and Christian Faith: Essays by Rudolf Bultmann and Others,* ed. Bernhard W. Anderson (London: SCM, 1964) 156.

Credits

"Texts That Linger, Words That Explode" was originally published in *Theology Today* 54 (1997) 180–99. Used by permission.

"Rereading the Book of Isaiah" was originally published under the name "Five Strong Rereadings of the Book of Isaiah" in *The Bible in Human Society: Essays in Honor of John Rogerson.* Edited by M. Daniel, R. P. Carroll, D. J. A. Clines, and P. R. Davies. JSOTSup 200. Sheffield: JSOT Press, 1995, 87–104. Used by permission.

"The Prophetic Word of God and History" was originally published in *Interpretation* 48 (1994) 239–51. Used by permission.

"The 'Baruch Connection': Reflections on Jeremiah 43:1-7" was originally published in *Journal of Biblical Literature* 113 (1994) 405–20. Used by permission.

"The Scandal and Liberty of Particularity" was originally published in a substantially different form as "Ecumenism as the Shared Practice of a Peculiar Identity" in *Word & World* 18 (1998) 122–35. Used by permission.

"Exodus in the Plural (Amos 9:7)" was originally published in *Many Voices, One God.* Edited by Walter Brueggemann and George Stroup. Louisville: Westminster John Knox, 1998. Used by permission.

6:22-23	56
8:8-13	11
8:13	11
11:16-17	11
15:2	118n20
21:5	49
23:7-8	112n39
23:16-22	48
26:16-19	54
23:16-17	48
29:11	56
31:28	53
31:31-34	10, 12
31:33	12
32	46
35	60
36	7ff, 46, 108n9
38:4	38
39:15-18	53
38:17-18	47f
42:18-22	48
42:8-17	49
42:9-17	47f
42:10-12	48
42:15b-17	48
42:16-17	48
43–44	53, 55, 74
43:10-13	49
43:10	53
43:11	118n20
43:23	52
43:1-7	46ff, 50
43:8—44:30	52f
43:8-13	52
44:1-23	49, 52
44:24-30	49, 52
44:30-31	49
45:1-5	53
45	46, 52f, 55
46–51	13, 53, 121n42
46:1-28	53
46:1-23	53
46:2	118n20
46:13	53, 118n20

46:19	53
46:26	53, 118n20
46:27-28	53
46	13, 53, 55, 57, 120n32
48:8-13	49
50–51	13, 54-57
50	56
50:1—51:58	53
50:2	14
50:31-32	14
50:41-42	56
50:43	14, 56
51:30	14
51:35-38	15
51:54-57	15
51:59-64	56
51:59	46
51:61	56
51:62	56
51:63	56
51:64	56
52	121n39

LAMENTATIONS
5:20	26

EZEKIEL
28:2	60
29:3	60
29-32	75
37:26	12

DANIEL
1	63

HOSEA
9:7	38

AMOS
1:3—2:16	93
1:3-5	97
2:4-5	93
2:6-26	93